DISTRICT FAMILY SURNAMES OF SCOTLAND

A companion book to
Scottish Clans And Their Associated Families

ROBERT J HESTON

ARCHWAY
PUBLISHING

Archway Publishing books may be ordered through booksellers or by contacting:

Archway Publishing
1663 Liberty Drive
Bloomington, IN 47403
www.archwaypublishing.com
844-669-3957

ISBN: 978-1-6657-4066-1 (sc)
ISBN: 978-1-6657-4067-8 (e)

Library of Congress Control Number: 2023905028

Print information available on the last page.

Archway Publishing rev. date: 04/17/2023

Acknowledgements

A book of this scope would not have been possible without the support and assistance of many people. I wish to acknowledge those fellow Council Of Scottish Clans and Associations (COSCA) researchers who persistently searched, with minimal successes, for all the surnames associated with Scotland and who encouraged me to publish a book like this after I finished Scottish Clans and Their Associated Families. It is also fitting that I acknowledge those individuals in clan societies and associations who also expressed interest in such a book to aid their support to visitors at a Scottish event find their connection to Scotland, even if there's no connection to their society or association.

To Suzanne Keifer, Clan Henderson Society, who willingly took the earlier manuscript for a test drive at the Stone Mountain Highland Games in October 2022. To Dennis Blythe, President Scottish District Families Association (SDFA), who test drove the final draft of the manuscript at the Central Florida Scottish Games in January 2023. Both of whom have read, used it in the field, and offered advice on the format, flow, and content of the book you see today.

My wife, Christi, who has been a source of constant support. This project might never have seen the light of day without her understanding and encouragement.

Two organizations I've seen firsthand do much of the "heavy lifting" assisting visitors to the Scottish games find their connection to Scotland are the Scottish District Families Association and Clan Henderson Society. The SDFA has dedicated their entire association to helping people find their connection to Scotland and have done so since the inception of their organization. Clan Henderson Society who always seems to have an individual at almost every game event going above and beyond in providing support to everyone searching their Scottish roots whether it's with their society or not.

Last, and not least, to my three kittens who each made extensive inputs trying to "rewrite" this manuscript each time my back was turned.

Contents

Introduction

This reference book, written to function as a stand-alone document, should be used in conjunction with those reference materials listed in the section titled Research Materials. Combined, these books will help you locate as much information as possible about any surname associated with Scotland being researched.

The use of the term "District" in the title, and throughout this book, is used loosely to identify the locations where records of the names included were recorded. I say that the term is used loosely only because the governing administrative areas identified as "District" and "Region" were done away with in Scotland around 1997. At that time these areas were redesignated as Councils, of which there are now 32. We in the Scottish-American community have yet to make that distinction.

Over the past 25 years that I have been associated with Scottish heritage events I've witnessed a great deal of effort being expended on refining and defining everything associated with Scottish Clans. However, with a couple of exceptions, little effort seems to have gone into giving the same amount of focus to the identification of surnames associated with Scotland who are not linked to a clan. This has been a problem for those of us who are attempting to help every visitor attending these events find their Scottish connection. Until now there has been little detailed, quality reference materials to adequately help us.

A necessary distinction to remember and share is the fact that there is a misperception that Scotland's people are centered strictly around the clan structure. Clans represent less than one third of all the people of Scotland. The non-clan families are city dwellers. They've not declared fealty to a clan chief, but provide goods, services, and labor in the regions in which they reside.

The information collected on this portion of Scotland's people comes from various publicly available sources such as Scottish government, regional administration, church (birth, marriage, death), and transportation (deportation) records. Regarding the latter source, there were no restrictions on the transportation of the subjects of England (English, Irish, Scots, Welsh) to the Americas, Caribbean, and Australia. Information extracted from these transportation records focused only on those transported prisoners specifically identified as Scottish. Prisoner transportation records to the Americas spanned the period 1600-1776 while those sent to Australia spanned the period 1776-1830.

As would be expected, the ravages of time has taken its toll on the availability of records prior to the middle 1700's. Census records available for review covered a limited period (1800-1921), and most church and parish records are not yet available on-line. Combine these issues with an apparent lack of interest in thoroughly documenting details about each prisoner transported prior to 1770 with information where they were born or lived at the time, left many gaps. After 1770 there appears to be a noticeable effort to provide greater detail on each person transported.

For prisoners transported to Australia, the gaps in information are more significant. The documents available provided a few additional names but, for the most part, copies of the microfiche records weren't legible enough to decipher information such as the country of the prisoner's origin making it difficult in determining if the names should be included here.

During my research there also appeared to be a strong indication that some Scottish family lines may have died out in Scotland as a direct result of transportation. A suspicion I believe is confirmed by the existence of the *Family Tree Y-DNA Project* whose aim is to identify descendants of the Scots captured in the battles of Dunbar and Worcester (1650-1651) and transported to the Americas Plantations.

Although political and religious reasons were grounds for transportation, for the most part transportation to the Americas and Australia took place to reduce overcrowding in prisons and on prison hulks. Crimes for those being transported ranged from assault, battery, sex crimes, adultery, bigotry, libel, rioting, threatening behavior, vagabonding, arson, deception (bankruptcy, forgery, fraud, perjury), and sundry crimes we would consider petty by today's standards. The periods of conflict with the English Crown attributed significantly to the numbers of those being transported. Conflicts such as the wars of the Three Kingdoms (1638-1651), the Covenanter Risings (1660-1680), Argyll's Rebellion (1685), and the Jacobite Rebellions (1715, 1719, and 1745) are periods in time bearing witness to greater numbers of prisoners being transported.

It is important to keep in mind that Scottish surnames were influenced by resident Picts, Norman invasion, Irish emigration in the 5th century, and Anglian immigrants along the borders. There were also raids and colonization of the Scottish Isles by the Norsemen some of which contributed to the surnames we see today. Generally, family lists ignored spelling variations which were a direct result of these migrations and subsequent urbanization occurring at a time when most of the people were illiterate.

Regarding spelling variations, one should not be inflexible over on the exact spelling of a family name when researching.

While this book lists nearly 10,000 names, it should not be considered a comprehensive reference document due to those gaps in information cited. However, as it stands now, this is the most comprehensive single source document we have today for those interested in assisting visitors to the Scottish heritage events who are interested in finding a surname connection to Scotland.

Errata
for the
2nd Edition, Scottish Clans And Their Associated Families

If you own a copy of this book, please note the following corrections:

There are two footnotes, (12) and (13) found against some names which are not found in the *Key To Footnotes*, pages xiii- xvii. Each of the names where the footnotes (12) and (13) are found should be changed to read (10).

The wording for all three references pointed to the same Clan Gordon notes of exception which indicates these names are accepted by Clan Gordon providing they met certain conditions. This corruption of data appeared to have happened sometime after the last manuscript was approved and before the book was printed.

Also note that the information regarding clans without chiefs, pages xiii and xx thru xxiii, as being Armigerous should be disregarded.

While researching the information to update this edition this term was found on several society and on the Standing Council of Scottish Chiefs (SCSC) website. Following publication of the book, while researching information for *District Family Surnames of Scotland*, I found those references are no longer present.

The SCSC and the Office of the Lord Lyon are adamant that a clan without a chief is not permitted by law to have arms which are only granted to an individual and not passed down to a group.

Suggested Research Materials

What's your name? What was your mother called? What was your father's mother's name? Most of us know at least a few of the surnames that make up the heritage of our own families. But what do these names mean and where did they come from?

To help you provide more detailed information to these questions, incorporate in your research materials at least these recommended materials. Each includes entries of the most common family names, with references to thousands more. Each gives a limited history of surnames, in many cases their original form, where they originated from and why it changed to what it is today.

1. *Scottish Clans and Their Associated Families* by Robert J. Heston
   A straightforward list of family names accepted by the individual Scottish Clans, Societies and Associations.

2. *District Family Surnames of Scotland* by Robert J. Heston
   A simple list of Scottish surnames, not affiliated with Scottish Clans, to include their Scottish region of origin.

3. *The Surnames of Scotland, Their Origin, Meaning and History* by George F. Black and Mary Elder Black
   The core of this work is a listing of surnames, each with a concise history and cross-references. Most of the names in *The Surnames of Scotland* match those *found in the District Family Surnames of Scotland*, with some exceptions. It is for those exceptions that I highly recommend using *The Surnames of Scotland* for cross referencing and researching names not found in *District Family Surnames of Scotland*.

4. *The Dictionary of English Surnames* by P.H. Reaney and R.M. Wilson
   As many names found in Scotland today do have their origins navigating there through England via the borders, this classic dictionary explains the origins of over 16,000 surnames.

5. *The Book of Ulster Surnames* by Robert Bell
   This book includes entries for over 500 of the most common family names found in Ulster.

6. *The Surnames of Ireland* by Edward MacLysaght
   Ireland was one of the earliest countries to evolve a system of hereditary surnames. More than 4,000 Gaelic Norman and Anglo-Irish surnames are listed in this book. Because of years of emigration, many Irish names are found in Scotland. This book, which was first published in 1957 and now is in its sixth edition, and remains the definitive record of Irish surnames, their genealogy, and their origins.

7. *The Surnames of Wales* by John and Sheila Rowlands
    According to the authors, there are many myths and misconceptions about surnames in Wales. How could there not be, when the ten most common nineteenth century surnames in Wales comprised nearly 56% of the population? Compare that to the ten most popular surnames in nineteenth century England accounted for less than 6% of that population. How does one identify their ancestors from all the others sharing the same name? This book attempts to rectify any misunderstanding about Welsh surnames.

8. *Tartans*, a three-volume set by William H. Johnston and Philip D. Smith, Jr. PhD
    A useful set of books to use when someone has a question about what their tartan looks like.

    In these three alphabetically arranged volumes, you will find over 1200 samples of vividly striped tartans covering the names Abbotsford to Yukon. Included is a brief historical background, definitions of related terms, and thread counts for the tartan weaver.

9. *District Tartans*, by Gordon Teall of Teallach and Philip D. Smith, Jr.
    District tartans, the authors argue, have at least as long a pedigree as clan tartans, but little attention has been paid to them over the last two centuries while interest has focused on clan tartans. In this book there are over fifty district tartans from Scotland and a similar number from abroad. The book also includes 21 state tartans from the USA.

Key Definitions And Term Of Usage

Much information has been compressed into as few pages as possible to reduce the cost of self-producing this book. The following should help to clear up any confusion there may be when first starting to use the data provided.

THE USE OF THE PREFIX MAC: While many family names have prefixes such as *M'*, *Ma*, *Mc*, *Mac*, *Mack*, and *O'*, each of these prefixes all mean "son of." For the purposes of expediting research and reducing the number of names, all prefixes, except *O'* and *Mack* have been converted to *Mac*. Remember to explain this to anyone you're helping research a family name.

SURNAMES:

Surnames were found in records from more than one region of Scotland. Rather than listing the same name several times with a different corresponding region in which records were found, it was decided to list the name once with an adjacent column providing a numerical identification for each region in Scotland in which the name appears. This example depicts how the district coding appears and is explained later. The key is found at Appendix-B.

SURNAME	DISTRICT
ASHER	5, 11, 42, 57, 76, 82

SURNAMES FOUND IN TRANSPORTATION RECORDS:

Prior to 1770, documentation was haphazard giving the appearance that there was a lack of interest in providing detailed information about the prisoners being deported. This resulted in a few instances where the only information available is the crime committed, if a battle took place the name of the battle and/or the place of capture, the year of transportation, and a two-letter designation indicating where the prisoner was transported to.

In rare cases the prisoner was identified as Scottish, the year transported, and the location they were transported to. Entries such as these are depicted with (NFI), meaning no further information, preceding all other information.

The two-letter identification in the "District" field indicates where a prisoner was deported to with AM = (Americas) and AU = (Australia). For those prisoners sent to the Americas, this could have been anywhere within the thirteen colonies or to one of the plantations in the Caribbean.

This example is an excerpt depicting how the transportation information appears.

SURNAME	DISTRICT
ASKING	JACOBITE, 1716, AM
BEAMES	ROYALIST, 1651, AM
CONAHER	JACOBITE, PRESTON, 1716, AM
GRISSELL	COVENANTER, 1685, AM
MILTOUN	(NFI) 1696, AM

DISTRICT/COUNTY CODES:

The use of a numeric identification for each location where a name was recorded was, as explained earlier, necessary to effectively use space. In the below example, the name Asher is found in six districts of Scotland. Each of these districts are identified with a numeric code as they are found in the decoding key in Appendix-B and depicted in the excerpt on the right.

SURNAME	DISTRICT
ASHER	5, 11, 33, 44, 58, 63

	DISTRICT
5	Argyll (*)
	(Forfarshire until 1928)
11	Banffshire (*)
33	Fife (*)
44	Inverness (*)
58	Moray (*) (Elginshire)
	(Elginshire until 1918)
63	Nairnshire (*) (Nairn)

SUGGESTED TARTANS:

Appendix-B also provides the key on how to decipher the coded information related to tartans which are suggested for wear. Using the district graphic information from above, the following breaks down how to determine the tartan suggested for wear.

An (*) following a district name identifies that a tartan by this district name exists and is the one suggested for wear.

	DISTRICT
5	Argyll (*)
	(Forfarshire until 1928)

An (*) followed by a (NUMBER) signifies a tartan is identified. The next parenthesis is the number of a separate district(s), listed in Appendix-B, that is the tartan suggested for wear.

	DISTRICT
63	Nairnshire (*) (57) (76) (81) (93)

An (*) followed by a (NAME) indicates a tartan is found for this district but not found in Appendix-B. When listed like this the suggested tartan will be found in Appendix-C.

		DISTRICT
58	Moray (*) (Elginshire)	

Appendix-C provides a brief description for each of the suggested tartans to include some history and any permissions required to weave or wear.

Understanding Scottish Surnames

General

Scottish surnames were influenced by resident Picts, Norman invasion, Irish emigration in the 5th century, and Anglian immigrants along the borders. There were also raids and colonization of the Scottish Isles by the Norsemen some of which contributed to the surnames we see today. Generally, family lists ignored spelling variations which were a direct result of these migrations and subsequent urbanization occurring at a time when most of the people were illiterate.

Regarding spelling variations, one should not be inflexible over on the exact spelling of a family name when researching. In his Expanded 9th Edition of *Tartan For Me!* Philip D. Smith, Jr., Ph.D., points out:

> *"Most of our ancestors were illiterate until recently especially if they were Gaelic speakers. Most Gaels were not taught to read or write their own language. In contrast with English, Gaelic speakers place more emphasis on the spoken language than on the written form. This means that Gaelic spelling is constantly being modified to match the spoken form, Irish in 1948 and Scottish Gaelic in 1982."*

Patronymics

Patronymics is where a son's name is derived from the father or an ancestor's forename, for example: Robert Heston's son Patrick would have been Patrick Robertson, and his son, in turn, would have been Hamish Patrickson. Thus, creating a challenge when researching family genealogy in that the surname changed with each successive generation.

The use of patronymic surnames was also passed down to the daughter with the girl adopting the father's forename and daughter applied to the end. Records show that the daughter suffix was commonly abbreviated, for example: Erin Robertsdaughter was then seen recorded as Robsdr, or Robsd.

The practice of using patronymic surnames died out in the Scottish Lowlands late in the 15th century when patronymic surnames, or surnames in general, were assumed as permanent family names. In the Highlands and Islands patronymic surnames continued in use well into the 18th and 19th centuries.

Territorial names, topographical names

Many surnames recorded in Scotland were those of nobles whose surnames were derived from the lands they possessed. These names are sometimes called territorial or habitation names. Many of these surnames were brought to Scotland by Anglo-Normans, whose surnames were derived from either land in Normandy or in England. For example, *Bruce* is derived from Brix in Manche, France. In the south of Scotland, *Barton* is derived from Dumbarton. Not all territorial surnames are derived from lands owned by their bearers. In some cases, such names were borne by tenants of the owners of the lands they lived on. In this way the bearers of these surnames may not have had any kinship with the landowners.

Then there are those Scottish surnames derived from geographical locations rather than specific places. These names refer to vague features like forests, streams, and marshes; such names may also refer to manmade structures such as castles and churches. Sometimes names derived from proper names of geographical features can be classified as topographic and refer to a location rather than a specific settlement.

Occupational names

Many surnames are derived from the occupations, or trades, of their original bearers. For example, *Shepherd*, *Mason*, and *Fletcher*. Eventually, true occupational surnames became hereditary and were passed down through families. Occupational names were rare amongst Gaelic speakers, examples of such surnames derived from Gaelic occupational name is *Gow*, from the Scottish Gaelic *Gobha* (smith), and *Macpherson* means "son of the parson", from the Gaelic surname *Mac a' Phearsain*.

Bynames

Bynames were once very common in Scotland. These names were used in areas where there were few names in circulation, and the bynames were added onto the name of a person, to distinguish them from others who bore the same name. Bynames were particularly prevalent in fishing communities in the northeastern part of Scotland but were also used in the Borders and the West Highlands. In some cases, such as fishing communities, the names of fishing boats were tacked onto the names of people.

Examples of Scottish surnames derived from nicknames are: *Little*, a nickname for a small man or the name was used to distinguish the younger of two bearers of the same personal name, and *White*, a descriptive name relating to someone with white or blonde hair, or complexion. One of the most common Scottish surnames is *Armstrong*, which means the son of a strong man.

Regional names, or ethnic names

Some Scottish surnames can be classified as either "regional names" or "ethnic names." These names originally referred to the origin of the bearer and tended to have been acquired by people who migrated a considerable distance from their original homes. In other cases, names were sometimes borne by people who were related to a foreign place. An example of an ethnic surname is Fleming, a native of Flanders, Belgium.

The use of formal surnames did not become common place until around the 12th century under the influence of Medieval English practice at which time it became common in the upper segments of Scottish society. Eventually the use of surnames became necessary to distinguish the common folk from the upper echelons by more than just the given name.

The Evolution Of Scottish Administrative Regions

For the most part, many of us have become accustomed to viewing the relationship of surnames in terms of *Clans, Districts, Shires, Provinces, Burghs,* and *Regions.* In the five latter cases, these government administrative designations have undergone numerous changes over the past 700 years.

The history of local government in Scotland is a complex tale of largely ancient and long established Scottish political units being replaced after the mid 20th century by a frequently changing series of different local government arrangements concluding with the terms "District" and "Region" being renamed "Councils."

Appendix-A provides a graphic overview of the changes having taken place between 1890 to the present day. The following is a short explanation of each administrative region.

PROVINCES: During the medieval period, government combined traditional kinship-based lordships with a relatively small system of royal offices. The dominant kindred were the Stewarts, who came to control many of the earldoms. Their acquisition of the crown, and a series of internal conflicts and confiscations, meant that by around the 1460s the monarchy had transformed its position within the realm, gaining control of most of the "provincial" earldoms and lordships. In the lowlands the crown was able to administer government through a system of sheriffdoms and other appointed officers, rather than semi-independent lordships.

SHIRES: The shires of Scotland have their origins in the sheriffdoms or shires over which a sheriff (a contraction of *shire reeve*) exercised jurisdiction.

BURGHS: A burgh is an autonomous municipal corporation in Scotland and Northern England, usually a city or town. This type of administrative division existed from the 12th century, when King David I created the first royal burghs. Burgh status was broadly analogous to borough status, found in the rest of the United Kingdom. Following local government reorganization in 1975, the title of "royal burgh" remains in use in many towns, but now has little more than ceremonial value.

COUNCILS: Between 1890 and 1975 local government in Scotland was organized with county councils (including four counties of cities). Between 1890 and 1929, there were parish councils and town councils, but with the passing of the Local Government (Scotland) Act of 1929, the functions of parish councils were passed to larger district councils and a distinction was made between large burghs and small burghs. This system was further refined by the passing of the Local Government (Scotland) Act 1947.

The Local Government (Scotland) Act of 1973 introduced a two-tier government in Scotland divided between large regional councils and small district councils. The only exceptions to this were the three island councils, Western Isles, Shetland, and Orkney, which had the combined powers of regions and districts. By 1997 these were abolished merging their powers into new unitary authorities. The new councils vary wildly in size – some are the same as counties, such as Clackmannanshire, some are the same as former districts, such as Inverclyde, and some are the same as the former regions, such as Highland.

The following list of Acts, with short summaries, provide a simple view of their impact on the definition and naming of regional governments in Scotland.

Acts of Parliament affecting Scottish government:

The **Local Government (Scotland) Act 1889** (52 & 53 Vict. c. 50) The main effect of the act was to establish elected county councils in Scotland.

The **Local Government (Scotland) Act 1894** (57 & 58 Vict. c. 58) Created a Local Government Board for Scotland and replaced existing parochial boards with parish councils.

The **Local Government (Scotland) Act 1929** (19 & 20 Geo 5 c. 25) Introducing joint county councils, large and small burghs and district councils.

The **Local Government (Scotland) Act 1947** (10 & 11 Geo. 6 c. 65) divided Scotland into counties, counties of cities, large burghs and small burghs, and landward areas (areas outside of burghs) of every county were divided into districts.

The **Local Government (Scotland) Act 1973** (c. 65) This Act made the most far-reaching changes to Scottish local government in centuries. It swept away the counties, burghs and districts which were largely based on units of local government dating from the Middle Ages and replaced them with a uniform two-tier system of regional and district councils (except in the islands, which were given unitary, all-purpose councils).

The **Local Government etc. (Scotland) Act 1994** (c. 39) is an Act of the Parliament of the United Kingdom which created the current local government structure of 32 unitary authorities covering the whole of Scotland. It abolished the two-tier structure of regions and districts which had previously covered Scotland except for the island's council areas. This Act also made provisions of naming a council (in Gaelic) shall be "*Comhairle*" with the addition of the name of their area.

The **Local Government (Gaelic Names) (Scotland) Act 1997** enables local councils in Scotland to rename the areas for which they are responsible with Gaelic names.

Armed Conflicts Resulting In Transportation

Although transportation of English, Irish, Scots, and Welsh prisoners to the Americas Plantations, and, after 1775, to Australia, were established to reduce overcrowding in prisons and on prison hulks, there was a significant surge in the numbers transported after each conflict with the Crown. The following is a brief summary of the most significant conflicts which resulted in a percentage of those Scots captured being transported. Only if those records recorded the nationality of the transported prisoner as Scottish were the names included in this book.

The Civil War of the Three Kingdoms
(SOURCE: https://military-history.fandom.com/wiki/Wars_of_the_Three_Kingdoms)

The English Civil War (1642–1651) was a series of armed conflicts and political problems between Parliamentarians (Roundheads) and Royalists (Cavaliers). The first (1642–46) and second (1648–49) civil wars pitted the supporters of King Charles I against the supporters of the Long Parliament, while the third war (1649–51) saw fighting between supporters of King Charles II and supporters of the Rump Parliament. The Civil War ended with the Parliamentary victory at the Battle of Worcester on 3 September 1651.

The Wars of the Three Kingdoms formed an intertwined series of conflicts taking place in England, Ireland, and Scotland after they came under the "Personal Rule" of the same monarch. The English Civil War is the best-known of these conflicts and included the execution of the Three Kingdoms' monarch, Charles I, by the English parliament in 1649. The wars were the outcome of tensions between king and subjects over religious and civil issues. Religious disputes centered on whether religion was to be dictated by the monarch or the choice of the subject, the subjects often feeling that they ought to have a direct relationship with God unmediated by any monarch or human intermediary. The related civil questions were to what extent the king's rule was constrained by parliaments — specifically his right to raise taxes and armed forces without consent.

The Battle of Dunbar (1650) – a battle of the *Third Civil War* fought largely on Scottish soil when Cromwell's English Parliamentary Army invaded Scotland. The Scottish Covenanters' army was heavily defeated by Cromwell at the Battle of Dunbar, and some 5,000 prisoners were marched south of the border by the Parliamentary army to Durham. Just 3,000 survived to be ordered into their temporary prison of Durham Cathedral, where many died from infection and fever. The order was given to transport the healthiest prisoners to the American colonies in New England and Virginia to undertake compulsory indentured labor.

The Battle of Worcester (1651) - A year to the day from Dunbar, the Royalist army under Charles II went down to its final defeat at Worcester, and again several thousand Scottish soldiers supporting Charles found themselves prisoners of war in England. Again, many were ordered for transportation. In one of many documented cases, the *John and Sarah* set sail with around 300 Scottish prisoners on board with 272 of them surviving to reach Charlestown.

Argyll's Rebellion (1685):
(Source: https://military-history.fandom.com/wiki/Argyll%27s_Rising)

More often known as Argyll's Rising, this was an attempt by a group of largely Scottish exiles, led by Archibald Campbell, 9th Earl of Argyll, to overthrow King James II and VII. It took place shortly before and in support of the Monmouth Rebellion, led by James Scott, 1st Duke of Monmouth. Argyll's Rising was intended to tie down Royal forces in Scotland while Monmouth's army marched on London. Both rebellions were backed by Protestants opposed to the kingship of James, a Roman Catholic.

Argyll, the chief of Clan Campbell, had hoped to raise several thousand men amongst his followers, while it was expected that many Presbyterians in southern Scotland would join the rebels. Argyll sailed from Holland with around 300 men, but on landing in Scotland attracted relatively few volunteers. Hampered by Argyll's inexperience as a commander, disagreements amongst the other leaders, and by an opposing force under the Marquess of Atholl, the rebels began to disperse in mid-June after an abortive invasion of Lowland Scotland. Most of their leaders were captured, including Argyll, who was executed.

Jacobite Rebellion:
(Source: https://military-history.fandom.com/wiki/Jacobite_risings)

These uprisings had the aim of returning James VII of Scotland and II of England, and later his descendants of the House of Stuart, to the throne of Great Britain after they had been deposed by Parliament during the Glorious Revolution. The series of conflicts takes its name from Jacobitism, from Jacobus, the Latin form of James.

The major Jacobite Risings were called the Jacobite Rebellions by the ruling governments. The "First Jacobite Rebellion" and "Second Jacobite Rebellion" were known respectively as "The Fifteen" and "The Forty-Five", after the years in which they occurred (1715 and 1745).

Although each Jacobite Rising had unique features, they were part of a larger series of military campaigns by Jacobites attempting to restore the Stuart kings to the thrones of Scotland and England (and after 1707, Great Britain). James was deposed in 1688 and the thrones were claimed by his daughter Mary II jointly with her husband, the Dutch-born William of Orange.

After the House of Hanover succeeded to the British throne in 1714, the risings continued, and intensified. They continued until the last Jacobite Rebellion ("the Forty-Five"), led by Charles Edward Stuart (the Young Pretender), who was soundly defeated at the Battle of Culloden in 1746. This ended any realistic hope of a Stuart restoration.

In time, many of those who survived transportation and their terms of indentured labor would settle in the colonies and have living descendants there today.

DISTRICT
FAMILY
SURNAMES
OF
SCOTLAND

SURNAME	DISTRICT	SURNAME	DISTRICT
ABBERLEY	52	ACHINFOUR	36
ABBEY	15, 20, 33	ACHINWALL	87
ABBIE	33	ACHLOCH	3
ABBOTTOUN	80	ACHMOOTY	33
ABE	75	ACHMOUR	37
ABEL	1, 36, 58	ACHMUTTIE	33
ABELL	36	ACHMUTTY	33
ABER	1	ACHNACH	85
ABERCHIRDER	42	ACKINHEVIE	67
ABERCORN	87	ACKINHEVY	67
ABERDALGEY	67	ACKLAND	80
ABERDALGIE	67	ACKLEY	44
ABERDALGIEY	67	ACKLIES	44
ABERDEEN	1, 47	ACKLY	44
ABERDEIN	1, 3	ACKMAN	8, 9, 26
ABERDENE	1	ACKWAITH	1
ABERDINE	1	ACKWARCHIE	1
ABERDORE	33	ACKWARCHY	1
ABERDOUN	33	ACOCK	3
ABERIGH	52	ACREE	44
ABERKIRDER	42	ACRES	71
ABERLADY	22	ACTON	44
ABERNETHIE	1, 8	ACUFF	75
ABERNIGHT	33	ACULTAN	36
ABERNYTE	33	ACULTANE	36
ABLE	36	ADAN	1
ABLETT	45	ADDISCOTT	67
ABRAHAM	84	ADEN	1
ABRAHAMSON	67	ADENS	1
ABRAM	84	ADIELL	1
ABRAMS	84	ADMISTON	35
ABSOLOM	75	ADOWELL	16
ABSOLON	75	AFFLECH	21
ABURDENE	1	AFFLICK	21, 28, 56
ACCO	87	AIDIE	8
ACHENBRUCK	85	AIKMAN	12, 17, 28
ACHENBRUIK	85	AIMER	3, 23, 28
ACHESON	42	AIMERS	12, 75, 77
ACHILES	80	AIMES	67
ACHINCLACH	68	AINSWORTH	20, 37, 67
ACHINCLOCH	68	AIRDRIE	3, 23, 89

SURNAME	DISTRICT	SURNAME	DISTRICT
AIRLY	8, 37, 49	AMOOTY	33
AIRMIT	33	AMOS	26, 75, 77, 87
AITCHESON	12, 26, 75	AMOSE	87
AITCHIESON	28, 56, 75	AMOUR	28, 33, 75
AITKINSON	49, 71, 75	AMOURS	33
AITKISON	8, 28, 56	ANALL	15
ALCHORN	56	ANCRET	22, 37
ALCORN	12, 23, 37	ANCRUM	23, 28, 56
ALDCORN	12, 28, 37, 75	ANDRES	71
ALDGIE	37, 50, 71	ANGUISH	3
ALDIE	1, 3	ANISON	36
ALEXR	1, 86	ANISOUN	36
ALEXT	89	ANKERS	23
ALFORD	37, 50, 71	ANKRET	1
ALGIE	37, 50, 71	ANNALL	33
ALICE	17, 47, 67	ANNAN	1, 23, 28, 33, 48, 67
ALISON	26, 28, 33, 71	ANNAND	1, 11, 28, 58, 67
ALISTER	28, 33, 89	ANNANDALE	3, 20, 47, 36
ALLASON	3, 8, 23	ANNAT	3, 23, 86
ALLATHAN	1	ANNECOMBE	75
ALLAWAY	16	ANNESLEY	2
ALLERDYCE	1, 8	ANNISTON	83
ALLES	48, 67	ANSTIE	44
ALLESTER	20, 33	ANSTY	44
ALLICE	17, 33, 88	ANTON	1, 11, 67
ALLIES	49, 67, 88	ANTONIO	28, 56
ALLOWAY	16	APPEL	44, 87
ALLS	67	APPLEBIE	87
ALMOND	3, 37, 88	APPLEBY	87
ALSTON	50, 67, 79, 88	APPLEGARTH	36
ALTON	JACOBITE, CARLISLE, 1747, AM	APPLETON	67
		APPLEYARD	21, 28, 89
ALTRIA	1	ARBECKIE	3
ALUDOCH	87	ARBIGLAND	36
ALVES	1, 47, 58	ARBLASTER	87
ALYNTON	35	ARBROATH	3
ALYTH	67	ARBUCKLE	3, 37, 50, 88
AMBLER	75	ARCHBELL	DUNBAR, 1650, AM
AMES	3, 33, 71	ARCHD	71
AMISFIELD	36	ARCHIE	1, 75
AMMOUS	87	ARCHMAN	28, 56

SURNAME	DISTRICT	SURNAME	DISTRICT
ARCHMORE	37	ARTHURLEE	68
ARCHMOUR	37	ARTHURSON	28, 56, 89
ARCUS	28, 56, 89	ARTLIE	67
ARDACH	36	ARTLY	67
ARDAUCH	36	ARTON	3
ARDENE	80	ARTOWN	3
ARDINCAPLE	83	ASH	23, 50
ARDLER	3	ASHBIE	87
ARDOCK	36	ASHBRIDGE	89
ARENS	28, 56, 89	ASHBY	87
ARGENT	87	ASHER	5, 11, 33, 44, 58, 63
ARGO	1, 56	ASHFORD	23
ARGYLL	5	ASHKIRK	37
ARHER	3	ASHWORTH	28, 55, 56
ARICARI	1	ASKALO	36
ARIES	36	ASKALOK	36
ARKINS	36	ASKBIE	22
ARKLAY	3	ASKBY	22
ARKLE	37, 47, 36, 50, 75	ASKEBY	22
ARKLEY	3, 23, 71, 88	ASKHAM	44
ARKLIE	3, 26, 28	ASKING	JACOBITE, 1716, AM
ARKLY	3, 8, 71	ASLOIS	8
ARMALIE	55	ASPINALL	23
ARMALY	55	ASPLEN	89
ARMAND	1	ASPLIN	89
ARMIT	3, 12, 33, 87	ASPLINDENE	67
ARMITT	87	ASSLESS	8
ARMOR	3, 37	ASTIE	36
ARMOUR	3, 5, 8, 50, 71	ATCHESON	21, 49, 89
ARNDLE	26	ATCHISON	21, 28, 75
ARNEIL	37, 50	ATHERAY	89
ARNELL	37, 50, 71	AUCHANSON	16
ARNOLD	28, 36, 75, 88	AUCHENBRUCK	85
ARNOULD	36	AUCHENCRAW	87
ARRAN	21	AUCHENLECK	JACOBITE, 1716, AM
ARRANTHREW	68	AUCHIE	89
ARRAS	67, 77	AUCHINACHIE	1
ARRAT	3	AUCHINACHY	1
ARRES	75, 77, 87	AUCHINHOVE	1
ARRIS	87	AUCHINMAD	30
ARSIL	1, 3	AUCHINMADE	30

SURNAME	DISTRICT	SURNAME	DISTRICT
AUCHINMAID	30	AYLIES	42
AUCHINMAIDE	30	AYLWARD	50
AUCHINROSS	83	AYMER	23, 47, 49
AUCHINTORE	68	AYMERS	3, 75
AUCHINTOUR	68	AYNEW	50
AUCHINTURE	68	AYRE	3, 8, 28, 77
AUCHINVOLE	37	AYSTON	JACOBITE, 1716, AM
AUCHINVOLE	50	BAAD	89
AUCHLYNE	87	BABTIE	20, 75
AUCHNIEVE	1	BACHELOR	3, 71, 75
AUCHTER	67	BACHOP	17, 50, 75, 89
AUCHTERBARDER	67	BACHOPE	75
AUCHTERBARNE	1	BACK	89
AUCHTERLONIE	33, 50, 88	BADGER	26, 37, 88
AUCHTERLONY	3, 33, 67	BAGAN	28, 37, 56
AUCHTERMONIE	87	BAGGRIE	1, 11
AUCKLAND	1, 11, 58, 67	BAGRIE	1, 11, 23
AUFRAYS	44	BAIGRIE	28, 56, 75
AUGHMUTIE	33	BAIKIE	15, 21, 67
AUGIE	44	BAILLIFF	49
AULD	8, 32, 48, 56, 70, 88	BAINSLIE	37
AULDJO	3	BAIRDEN	21, 36, 49
AULDMILL	87	BAIRDON	36
AULDOTH	87	BAIRDONE	36
AULDS	67	BAIRNER	36
AULDTON	75	BAIRNSFEATHER	22, 32
AULNOY	37	BAIRNSON	37, 50, 89
AULT	67	BAISLER	62
AUMBLER	75	BAKER	1, 28, 47
AUSTIE	45	BAKEY	3
AUTRAY	3	BAKIE	15, 56, 67, 75
AUTRIE	3	BALANTINE	8, 67, 75
AUTRY	3	BALANTYNE	56, 67, 75
AVENER	87	BALANWALL	33
AVERY	87	BALARDIE	3, 23
AWBUFN	87	BALCAIRN	67
AWELL	3	BALCAIRNIE	67
AXON	68	BALCAIRNY	67
AYCOCK	3	BALCATHIE	3
AYLEBET	67	BALCATHY	3
AYLEBOT	67	BALCHRISTIE	62

SURNAME	DISTRICT	SURNAME	DISTRICT
BALCHRISTY	62	BALLINDALLOCH	85
BALCHRO	3	BALLINGAL	23, 28, 33
BALCKLIE	36	BALLINTINE	21, 50, 71
BALCOMEY	33	BALLS	3, 23, 47
BALCONQUALL	33	BALLSILLIE	33
BALCUMLIE	1	BALMAIN	1, 3, 28, 33, 67
BALCUMLY	1	BALMAN	28, 75, 89
BALD	17, 26, 50, 67	BALMANNO	28
BALDEN	23, 26, 67	BALMANO	67
BALDERNIE	1	BALMARINO	6, 75
BALDERNY	1	BALMER	12, 67, 75
BALDERSTON	14, 20, 32, 68, 89	BALMOSSIE	3
BALDERSTOUN	32	BALMOSSY	3
BALDIE	33	BALMYLE	3
BALDIE	89	BALMYLES	3
BALDOWNIE	3	BALNDENNIE	33
BALDOWNY	3	BALNDENNY	33
BALDRAINIE	87	BAMBER	17, 26, 71
BALDRAINY	87	BAMBERRY	28, 56
BALDRANIE	87	BANBRIDGE	8, 33
BALDRANY	87	BAND	33, 67, 89
BALDRO	3	BANDEEN	1
BALDWIN	15, 23, 26, 36	BANES	33, 67
BALDY	3, 23, 33	BANK	DUNBAR, 1650, AM
BALERNO	87	BANKE	DUNBAR, 1650, AM
BALGONIE	1	BANKER	89
BALGONY	1	BANKES	87
BALGREEN	68	BANKIE	37, 50
BALHARDIE	67	BANN	36
BALHARDY	67	BANNAN	28, 75, 89
BALHARRIE	3, 23, 67	BANNATINE	8, 37, 71
BALHARRY	3, 67	BANNIGAN	28, 56, 89
BALHARY	3, 23	BANNISTER	67, 88, 89
BALINGALL	28, 33, 71	BANNYTINE	28, 37, 50
BALLANIE	87	BANSLIE	1773, AM
BALLANTYRE	50	BAPTIE	67, 75, 77, 87
BALLANY	87	BAPTY	87
BALLENIE	87	BAR	1, 8, 50
BALLENY	87	BARBAR	8, 11, 26
BALLEW	1	BARCKLAY	1, 33
BALLIE	26, 48, 86	BARCLY	56

SURNAME	DISTRICT	SURNAME	DISTRICT
BARDNER	28, 33, 48, 87	BARTLEMAN	67, 71
BARENBER	36	BARTLEMORE	8, 71
BARFOOT	68	BARTLETT	1, 2, 11
BARGARNIE	22	BARTLEY	12, 45, 89
BARGARNY	22	BARTRAM	12, 26, 67
BARGILL	37	BASSENDEAN	22
BARHAM	1	BASSENDEN	22
BARHILL	83	BASSILLIE	33
BARKER	28, 33, 77, 89	BASSILLY	33
BARLACK	89	BASSON	1, 37
BARLAND	8, 24, 71	BASTOW	44
BARLAS	37, 50, 67	BATCHELOR	3, 23, 33, 62, 87
BARLASS	3, 33, 67	BATE	1, 3, 47
BARLEMAN	87	BATES	28, 56, 89
BARLOCK	89	BATESON	20, 71, 89
BARLOW	11, 33, 37	BATHGATE	12, 26, 75, 77
BARNABIE	75	BATHIE	3, 23, 33
BARNABY	75	BATHISON	67
BARNBIE	75	BATHLE	67
BARNBY	75	BATTEN	5
BARNES	21, 71, 75	BATTERSBY	37, 49, 67
BARNETT	1, 45, 47, 56, 67	BATTES	3
BARNFEATHER	32	BATTIESON	89
BARNS	8, 12, 21, 50, 88	BATTISON	20, 67, 89
BARNSDALE	3	BATTLE	36, 89
BARNSFEATHER	22	BAUCHOP	17, 75, 88, 89
BARNSON	89	BAUCHOPE	37, 75, 88, 89
BARNTON	62	BAULD	20, 37, 89
BARNWELL	36	BAULDIE	3, 23
BARNY	15	BAWES	67
BARRACK	1, 21	BAY	14, 33, 37
BARRAS	56, 67, 89	BAYLISS	14
BARRETT	23, 28, 89	BAYSLER	62
BARRIDGE	8	BEAD	33, 89
BARRONS	28, 33, 56	BEADIE	11, 21, 47
BARROW	1, 26, 56, 58	BEAKEY	3
BARROWMAN	28, 37, 50	BEAMES	ROYALIST, 1651, AM
BARTER	3, 67, 89	BEANSTON	22
BARTLAM	44	BEANSTOUN	22
BARTLE	54	BEARDEN	49
BARTLEMA	26	BEARUP	12, 56, 75

SURNAME	DISTRICT	SURNAME	DISTRICT
BEAT	3, 23, 33	BEITHE	26
BEATLE	1, 75, 77	BELCHER	28, 56
BEATS	50	BELCHES	75
BEATSON	20, 33, 48, 56	BELFIELD	26, 56
BEATTON	56	BELFORD	3, 20, 28, 47, 49, 56, 87
BEAVER	71	BELHAVEN	50
BEAVERLY	1, 47	BELHELVIE	1
BEBBER	87	BELHELVY	1
BEBER	87	BELINDA	33
BECHER	44	BELLEW	1
BECK	21, 36, 37, 49	BELLHOUSE	37
BECKET	8, 37, 71	BELLMAN	87
BECKETT	28, 33, 75, 89	BELLS	8, 70, 89
BECKIE	33, 37, 75	BELLY	3, 89
BECKTON	36	BELTEN	22
BEDDIE	3, 36	BELTIE	1
BEDDY	3, 36	BELTIN	22
BEDEFORD	37	BELTMAKER	87
BEDFORD	37	BELTON	22, 67, 88
BEECH	2, 36, 49	BELTY	1
BEECHAM	37, 50, 52	BEMBS	28
BEECHEM	52	BEME	WORCESTER, 1651, AM
BEEDLE	1, 23, 47	BENDALL	21, 49, 75
BEEDLES	1	BENDLOW	1
BEER	87	BENGAL	33
BEERE	WORCESTER, 1651, AM	BENHAM	54
BEERHOPE	56, 75	BENHOPE	56
BEERUP	56	BENIGAN	87
BEESTON	87	BENIGNO	87
BEET	28, 33, 56	BENNE	WORCESTER, 1651, AM
BEG	1, 11, 48	BENNET	11, 17, 44, 48, 75
BEGBIE	26, 28, 67, 75	BENNETT	11, 23, 33, 44, 50, 75
BEGBY	75	BENNIE	17, 88, 89
BEGG	JACOBITE, PRESTON, 1716, AM	BENNOCH	21, 28, 36, 89
		BENNY	20, 67, 89
BEGLEY	37, 50, 71	BENSON	37, 71, 75, 89
BEGLY	15	BENT	83
BEGRIE	1, 56	BENTLEY	5, 37, 50
BEID	28, 58, 67	BENTON	1
BEITCH	87	BENVIE	3, 23, 67
BEITH	14, 48, 71	BENVIES	23

SURNAME	DISTRICT	SURNAME	DISTRICT
BENVIY	23	BIDUNE	75
BENVIYS	23	BIDY	1
BENZIE	1, 47	BIE	3
BENZIES	1, 11, 47, 58	BIGAM	20, 71, 87, 89
BENZY	1	BIGBEE	75
BENZYS	1	BIGBIE	75
BERE	87	BIGEAM	36, 87
BEREERE	5	BIGG	1, 33, 71
BEREFORD	32	BIGGAM	20, 49, 89
BERFORD	32	BIGGAR	49, 67, 77, 83
BERLIE	3, 47	BIGGARS	83
BERNARD	17, 33, 56	BIGGART	8, 14, 20, 68
BERNER	33	BIGGS	28, 49, 56
BERNHAM	87	BIGHAM	8, 14, 49, 87
BERTIE	3, 28, 47	BIGLAND	20, 67, 89
BERTON	33, 87	BIGLIE	87
BERTRAM	12, 26, 67, 87	BIGLY	87
BERWICK	12, 23, 22, 33, 56, 87	BILBY	21
BESSIT	28, 33, 56	BILHAM	52
BEST	67, 75, 77, 87	BILLET	67
BETAGH	36	BILLHOPE	75
BETHEL	44	BILLIE	87
BETHELL	44	BILLINGTON	21, 37, 75
BETSON	17, 48, 67	BILLY	87
BETSY	67	BILSAND	20, 37, 89
BETTS	3, 23, 89	BILSLIE	1773, AM
BEVAN	8, 21	BILSTON	5
BEVERLEY	1, 47	BILSTONE	5
BEVERLIE	87	BILSTUN	5
BEVERLY	1, 67, 87	BILSTUNE	5
BEWICK	33, 50, 68	BILTON	67, 75, 89
BEWS	2, 15, 28, 56, 67	BINGHAM	28, 67, 71
BICHAM	52	BINGS	1, 47
BICHENO	85	BINNY	3, 67, 88
BICKERSTAFF	8, 26, 89	BIRCH	21, 28, 50, 87
BICKERTON	75	BIRD	8, 12, 26, 87, 88
BICKET	8, 71, 75	BIRDS	8
BIDDIE	1	BIRKENSHAW	68
BIDDY	1	BIRKETT	28, 49, 56
BIDIE	1, 11	BIRKMEIR	36
BIDUN	75	BIRKMIRE	36

SURNAME	DISTRICT	SURNAME	DISTRICT
BIRKMYER	36	BLADDERS	1
BIRKMYRE	36, 37, 49, 71,	BLAICKIE	67, 75, 77
BIRNAM	67	BLAIND	36
BIRNEY	1, 89	BLAINEY	37, 50, 89
BIRNHAM	67	BLAIRFORD	67
BIRNIE	1, 23, 50	BLAKELY	8, 28, 86
BIRREL	21, 23, 33	BLAKENEY	14
BIRRELL	21, 33, 48	BLAKIE	12, 75, 88
BIRRILL	33, 50, 80	BLAMIRE	36
BIRT	50	BLAN	5, 37, 71
BISAT	33	BLANCH	37, 50
BISCUT	37	BLAND	8, 21, 49, 50, 71
BISCUTT	37	BLANDELL	(NFI) AM
BISHOP	28, 44, 50, 56, 88	BLANEY	50
BISLAND	20, 37, 71	BLANK	15
BISSLAND	37, 71, 89	BLANKIN	3
BITACK	45	BLANTYRE	83
BITTLESTON	STIRLING, 1773 AM	BLARE	33
BITTRIDGE	34	BLEAK	75
BLABER	1	BLEAKIE	56, 75
BLABURN	33	BLEAN	37
BLACHRIE	1, 75	BLELLOCH	33, 67
BLACKALL	1	BLELLOCK	67
BLACKBELL	12, 26	BLELOCH	17, 33
BLACKBURN	14, 37, 44, 50, 67, 71	BLELOCK	67
BLACKE	WORCESTER, 1651, AM	BLENKINSOP	36
BLACKENWALL	33	BLENNIE	37, 60
BLACKET	12, 36, 37, 58	BLIGH	23
BLACKHALL	1, 12, 26	BLINDSEIL	1
BLACKIT	17	BLINDSELL	1
BLACKLAW	21, 47, 67	BLOCCAR	32
BLACKLAWS	3, 26, 47	BLOCKER	32
BLACKLEY	21, 36, 49, 50	BLOCKKER	32
BLACKLIE	5, 8, 71	BLOMFIELD	23
BLACKMAN	36	BLOOMFIELD	28, 33, 50
BLACKSHAW	36	BLOUNT	21, 37, 49
BLACKSTOCKS	8, 21, 67	BLOWER	83
BLACKSTONE	36, 68	BLUEFIELD	44
BLACKTON	87	BLUES	3, 23, 47
BLACKWATER	1	BLUND	80
BLACKWELL	28, 36, 56, 89	BLUNTACH	45, 58

SURNAME	DISTRICT	SURNAME	DISTRICT
BOA	14, 21, 35, 75, 77	BON	21, 50, 71
BOAG	48, 71, 88, 89	BONALIE	33
BOAK	28, 56, 88	BONALLIE	87
BOASE	3, 23, 44	BONALLO	33
BOATH	3, 23, 48	BONALLY	87
BOAX	56	BOND	37, 50, 56
BOCHANAN	5	BONELLA	3, 23, 48
BODAN	8, 49, 89	BONELLY	33, 87
BODDAN	8, 49, 89	BONES	33, 50, 68
BODDEN	36	BONESS	49
BODDIE	1, 89	BONHILL	37
BODDON	49, 89	BONK	44
BODELL	83	BONMAN	3
BODEN	49, 88, 89	BONNIMAN	1, 11
BODIE	1, 11, 28	BONNINGTON	21, 32, 56, 77
BODY	1	BONNYMAN	2
BODYS	1	BONVILLE	13
BOE	21, 67, 75, 87	BOOG	28, 48, 56, 89
BOGAN	23, 37, 71	BOOGE	28
BOGGIE	1, 21, 33	BOOKER	11
BOGIE	17, 33, 48, 83	BOOKLASS	28, 37, 50
BOGRIE	36	BOOKLESS	12, 26, 75
BOGRY	36	BOON	8, 38, 89
BOKE	89	BOOSIE	33
BOLAM	75	BOOTH	1, 2, 11, 21
BOLAN	50, 71, 88	BOOTHMAN	28, 56, 89
BOLAND	20, 37, 50	BOOTHROYDE	50, 67
BOLD	12, 33, 77, 35	BOOTLE	85
BOLDON	52	BORDER	67, 89
BOLE	1	BORELAND	8, 48, 67
BOLES	1, 67	BORER	1
BOLLAN	5	BORHILL	83
BOLLAND	5	BORIE	67
BOLLARD	80	BORLUND	68
BOLLEN	5	BORRIE	14, 23, 67, 68
BOLLIN	5	BORROWMAN	3, 67, 88, 89
BOLLING	5	BORRY	68
BOLMAR	37	BORTHFIELD	87
BOLMER	37	BORTHICK	26, 28, 56
BOLT	33, 35, 50, 89	BORWICK	33, 67
BOLTON	12, 26, 50, 75, 87	BOSKILL	37, 50

SURNAME	DISTRICT	SURNAME	DISTRICT
BOSS	33, 48, 67	BOYACK	1, 3, 23
BOSSWELL	20	BOYDEN	75
BOSTACK	87	BOYE	WORCESTER, 1652, AM
BOSTICK	87	BOYLAN	28, 56
BOSTON	12, 21, 31, 45, 75	BOYN	1, 58, 89
BOSWEL	17, 33	BOYS	21, 63, 89
BOTHIE	1	BRABAND	DUNBAR, 1650, AM
BOTHWELL	1, 47, 83	BRABONER	19
BOTHY	1	BRACE	36
BOTTOMLEY	17, 71	BRACK	12, 20, 22, 75
BOTTOMLY	87	BRACKENRIDGE	8, 37, 50, 83
BOUCHER	20, 33, 37	BRACKHAWK	1
BOUG	56	BRACO	87
BOUGLAS	50, 75	BRACON	33
BOUIE	11, 37, 89	BRADE	36
BOULTON	44	BRADFORD	12, 33, 50
BOUND	54	BRADING	74, 68
BOUNDS	54	BRADLIE	75
BOUNTIFF	3	BRADNER	87
BOURHILL	56, 71, 83	BRADSHAW	28, 49, 50, 87
BOURKE	3, 20, 23	BRAE	28, 56, 67
BOURNE	1, 37	BRAES	79, 88
BOUSIE	23, 33, 67, 88	BRAID	26, 33, 87, 88
BOUSY	67	BRAIDEN	28, 36, 37, 49,
BOUTHORN	75	BRAIDFOOT	36
BOUX	56	BRAIDFOOTE	36
BOW	17, 37, 82, 84, 89	BRAIDIE	28
BOWDEN	3, 28, 56, 87	BRAIDON	36
BOWE	28, 56, 67, 84	BRAIDWOOD	23, 28, 50, 56, 89
BOWEN	14, 17, 75	BRAIK	1, 28
BOWES	8, 71, 85, 88	BRAITHWAITE	87
BOWHILL	12, 26, 75	BRAKENRIDGE	5, 8, 89
BOWICK	3, 37, 47	BRAKHAUGH	1
BOWIS	67	BRALAND	8
BOWLBIE	52	BRAMBE	42
BOWLBY	52	BRAMBEY	42
BOWLING	5	BRAMBIE	42
BOWNESS	21	BRAMLEY	89
BOWSER	88	BRAMWELL	21, 75, 88
BOWYER	44	BRAN	36
BOY	WORCESTER, 1652, AM	BRANAN	20, 23, 71, 82, 89

SURNAME	DISTRICT	SURNAME	DISTRICT
BRANCH	1	BREWIS	3, 12
BRAND	3, 47, 48	BREYMER	54
BRANDAN	80	BRIAN	36
BRANDEN	80	BRICHANAN	50
BRANDER	1, 42, 11, 58	BRICHEN	1, 3, 37
BRANDS	1, 58, 89	BRICKNALL	3, 23
BRANDY	1, 11	BRIDEN	21, 26, 47
BRANKIN	23	BRIDGE	15, 36, 37, 50
BRANKS	20, 56, 89	BRIDGEFORD	1, 47, 67, 89
BRANNAN	21, 23, 37, 50	BRIDGES	8, 26, 28, 33
BRANNEN	33, 37, 89	BRIDIN	44
BRANNON	23, 37	BRIDSON	36
BRANZEAN	87	BRIERCLIFF	36
BRATNEY	36	BRIERCLIFFE	36
BRATNIE	36	BRIGG	1
BRATTON	36	BRIGGS	1, 26, 48, 49
BRAVAND	DUNBAR, 1650, AM	BRIGHAM	22
BRAVENDER	DUNBAR, 1650, AM	BRIGHTON	5, 23, 67
BRAY	1, 20, 50, 89	BRIGS	12, 37, 50
BRAYDEN	36	BRIGTON	50
BRAYDON	36	BRIM	86
BREADING	74	BRIMBER	89
BREADY	20, 23, 37	BRIMER	33
BREAKENRIDGE	5, 8, 14,	BRIMS	15, 28, 86, 89
BREAKHAUGH	44	BRINDEL	44
BREAKHAWK	44	BRINDELL	44
BREAKIE	44	BRINDLE	28, 44, 56
BREAKY	44	BRINGLE	77
BRECK	36	BRINTON	83
BREE	23, 37, 50, 71	BRISBAND	50
BREEDEN	23	BRISBON	68
BREEN	23, 37, 50, 71	BRISBONE	68
BREID	36	BRISTOW	44
BREINGAN	17, 20, 48	BRITAIN	37, 50, 89
BREMER	3, 23, 88	BRITCHER	1
BREMNAR	3, 15, 28	BRITTAIN	50
BRENDAN	JACOBITE, 1716, AM	BRITTEN	37, 50
BRENNAN	3, 23, 37, 50, 71	BRITTON	21, 50, 71
BRESSACK	3	BROA	68
BREW	1, 3, 67	BROACH	21, 49, 50
BREWHOUSE	67	BROAD	48, 67, 75

SURNAME	DISTRICT	SURNAME	DISTRICT
BROADDIE	17	BROUNELL	WORCESTER, 1652, AM
BROADFOOT	21, 26, 49, 67, 89	BROUNLEE	28, 71, 75
BROADLEE	44	BROW	3, 21, 67
BROADLEY	20, 37, 44, 50	BROWLEY	50
BROADLIE	21, 44, 71, 89	BROWNFIELD	75
BROADWOOD	26, 67, 77	BROWNHILLS	87
BROATCH	21, 49, 50	BROWNIE	1, 47
BROBBEL	87	BROWNLEA	45, 50
BROBBLE	87	BROWNRIG	49
BROCK	15, 67, 88	BRUNELL	5
BROCKET	83	BRUNILL	5
BROCKETT	83	BRUNLIE	87
BROCKEY	71	BRUNLY	87
BROCKHOUSE	87	BRUNTFIELD	3, 23, 67, 87
BROCKIE	67, 75, 77	BRUNTON	3, 67, 75, 77, 87
BROCKLEBANK	37, 50	BRUNTOUN	3, 87
BROCKLEY	56, 88	BRYAN	8, 20, 49, 56
BRODERICK	44	BRYANS	8, 37, 83
BRODY	5, 20, 67	BRYANT	16
BROGAN	1, 37, 71, 89	BRYDEN	74, 21, 77, 87
BROKE	67, 71, 86	BRYDON	67, 75, 77
BROLL	89	BRYDONE	28, 49, 75
BROLLY	36	BRYDSON	47, 49, 71
BROMLEY	28, 67, 89	BRYMAN	23
BROODIE	1, 33, 75	BRYMER	82
BROOK	1, 26, 67	BRYSON	20, 26, 37, 83
BROOKE	1	BRYSSON	28, 56, 67
BROOKER	79	BUBB	3
BROOKES	1	BUCH	44
BROOKFIELD	50	BUCHANNAN	5, 20, 67
BROOKS	26, 56, 89	BUCHART	1, 33
BROOM	8, 36, 86, 88, 89	BUCHNER	44
BROOME	37, 50	BUCKANEN	WORCESTER, 1652, AM
BROOMFIELD	12, 26, 56, 75, 87	BUCKANON	WORCESTER, 1652, AM
BROOMHILL	36	BUCKHAM	12, 75, 77, 87
BROOMSIDE	3	BUCKHOLM	75
BROTCHY	86	BUCKLE	26, 28, 67, 87
BROTHERS	62	BUCKLEW	1
BROTHERSTON	12, 26, 35, 75	BUCKLEY	23, 37, 50
BROTHERSTONE	12, 71, 75	BUCKNER	1, 44
BROUCH	3, 67	BUDDS	33

SURNAME	DISTRICT	SURNAME	DISTRICT
BUDERICK	7	BURD	28, 67, 88, 89
BUGES	87	BURDETT	37, 44, 50
BUGG	28, 56, 67	BURDETTE	44
BUGLAS	88	BURGAN	12, 67
BUGLASS	12, 50, 87	BURGAR	67, 89
BUICK	3, 23, 67	BURGER	45, 67, 89
BUISSLAND	89	BURGES	11, 58, 89
BUITTLE	36	BURGESS	1, 21, 45, 58, 89
BULKENWALL	33	BURGH	37, 50, 67
BULL	37, 44, 68, 81, 89	BURGHER	44
BULLEN	87	BURGOYNE	37, 50, 67
BULLENS	87	BURLEIGH	47, 88
BULLER	17, 67, 88	BURLEY	1, 47, 68, 88
BULLERSWELL	75	BURLIE	1, 11, 47
BULLIANS	67	BURLIEGH	1
BULLIN	67	BURMAN	3, 23, 47
BULLINS	67	BURNE	87
BULLION	8, 37, 70, 89	BURNEVILLE	36
BULLIONS	3, 33, 67, 89	BURNEY	8, 47, 89
BULLOCK	3, 28, 89	BURNFIELD	8, 37, 67
BULLS	44, 68	BURNHAM	54, 67
BULLSON	75	BURNHEM	54, 67
BULLYMORE	67	BURNIE	21, 49, 89
BULMAN	21, 26, 75	BURNMAN	3, 23, 67
BULMAR	37	BURNSIDE	26, 37, 50
BULMER	37	BURNTFIELD	67
BUNCH	3, 23, 67	BURNVILLE	36
BUNCHRAW	44	BURNY	3, 28, 56, 87
BUNNEY	33	BURR	1, 54, 11
BUNNIS	68	BURRARD	50
BUNNY	1, 47, 87	BURREL	12, 33, 89
BUNY	87	BURRELL	28, 33, 56
BUNYAN	1, 28, 56, 75	BURROUGHS	28, 37, 56
BUNYIE	87	BURROWS	37, 49, 50
BUNZEON	1	BURRY	3, 23, 58
BURBANK	87	BURSICK	JACOBITE, 1716, AM
BURBEAN	DUNBAR, 1650, AM	BURTON	12, 26, 77
BURBEEN	DUNBAR, 1650, AM	BURTT	33, 67
BURBIE	8, 37, 49	BURY	28, 37, 89
BURBONE	87	BUSBIE	68
BURCH	3, 75, 87, 89	BUSBY	68

SURNAME	DISTRICT	SURNAME	DISTRICT
BUSHNELL	3, 37, 50	CAIREY	3, 28, 37
BUSSEY	33	CAIRG	36
BUTCHARD	1, 3, 23, 28	CAIRN	23, 88, 89
BUTCHART	1, 3, 23, 67	CAIRNCROSS	3, 23, 26
BUTCHER	1, 3	CAIRNES	56
BUTHE	44	CAIRNIE	33, 36, 67, 71
BUTHLAY	1	CAIRNOCHAN	89
BUTLER	28, 56, 67, 87	CAIRNS	17, 45, 50, 67, 75
BUTT	1, 37, 50	CAIRNY	36, 67
BUTTLER	12, 28, 67	CAIRSTAIRS	33, 48
BUTTON	12, 28, 67	CAIRT	50
BUTTRESS	44	CALANON	67
BUY	84	CALCOTT	15
BUYTH	44	CALDCOTT	35
BUZBY	68	CALDECOTT	35
BYATS	87	CALDERHEAD	20, 28, 33, 83
BYDON	75	CALDERWOOD	8, 20, 67, 68, 83
BYDONE	75	CALDOW	8, 21, 49
BYDSON	36	CALDWALL	8, 49, 71
BYE	3, 87	CALDWEL	5, 71
BYOOT	37	CALEY	33
BYRNE	1, 20, 89	CALLACK	36
BYRON	11, 17, 89	CALLAGHAN	23, 37, 50, 56
CABEL	3	CALLAND	49
CABELL	3	CALLEND	37
CABLE	1, 3, 23	CALLENDAR	49, 77, 89
CADDEL	20, 67	CALLIE	33, 36
CADDEN	35	CALLIGHAN	28, 37, 56
CADDENHEAD	1, 11, 47	CALLNOR	67
CADDIN	35	CALLOCHAN	56
CADENHEAD	1, 47, 36	CALLY	33, 49, 77
CADGER	1, 3, 23, 67	CALNON	67
CADIEN	67	CALTON	1, 33, 36
CADZEON	87	CALVERT	21, 67, 75
CADZOW	8, 50, 88	CALVIN	37, 49, 50
CAFFERTY	8, 20, 21	CAMBELL	3, 23, 67
CAFFRAY	67	CAMBIE	36
CAGAN	45	CAMBRO	33
CAGLE	37, 50, 89	CAMBY	36
CAHILL	28, 56	CAMMOCK	36
CAIE	1, 47	CAMPAIGN	50

SURNAME	DISTRICT	SURNAME	DISTRICT
CAMPBLE	45, 71, 89	CARDNO	1
CAMPSIE	28, 67, 71, 89	CARELTON	56
CAMPSY	89	CARFRAE	28, 56, 75
CANADE	DUNBAR, 1650, AM	CARGIL	3
CANDEL	87	CARIN	36
CANDELL	87	CARKETTLE	87
CANDEN	1	CARL	2
CANDIN	1	CARLAN	1, 87
CANDLISH	8, 36, 49, 89	CARLE	1, 2, 26, 89
CANDO	8	CARLEN	21, 23, 49
CANDON	1	CARLEY	8, 45, 71
CANDOW	3, 23, 67	CARLILE	26, 71, 89
CANDWELL	5	CARLIN	8
CANE	15, 23, 37	CARLINE	37, 50, 71
CANFIELD	37, 50	CARLING	28, 56
CANMORE	15, 67	CARLNOR	67
CANNAL	8, 71, 89	CARLOW	28, 33, 71
CANNELL	WORCESTER, 1652, AM	CARLTON	56
CANNEY	37, 50, 89	CARLYLE	21, 49, 75
CANNING	37, 63, 71	CARMAC	3
CANNOCH	87	CARMACK	3
CANNON	5, 20, 49	CARMAIG	3
CANOCK	87	CARMAN	75
CANON	1, 28, 56	CARMELL	3
CANS	8, 33	CARMEN	75
CANSO	23	CARMICHEAL	5, 17, 75
CANSOW	23	CARMMAN	87
CANTLEY	1, 56, 58, 67	CARMON	87
CANTLIE	1	CARMONT	75
CANTLY	11, 15, 58	CARNACHAN	8, 71, 89
CANVIN	82	CARNAHAN	8, 21, 37
CAPEL	67	CARNBY	33
CAPPAR	1	CARNDUFF	8, 71
CARABINE	34	CARNERON	50
CARAN	89	CARNES	56
CARBERRY	87	CARNIGAL	1
CARCARIE	67	CARNIGUL	1
CARCARY	67	CARNOCHAN	37, 49, 89
CARCHARIE	47	CARNOCK	36
CARDEAB	3	CARNON	49
CARDIE	1, 71, 89	CARNWATH	36

SURNAME	DISTRICT	SURNAME	DISTRICT
CARON	89	CARVELL	3
CARPENTER	1, 12, 67, 88	CARVER	3, 23, 67
CARPHIN	28, 56, 88	CARVISION	44
CARPOL	37	CARWARDINE	68
CARPOLE	37	CARWELL	68
CARRAIL	26, 56, 89	CARWOOD	83
CARRELL	37, 50, 89	CARY	3, 28, 37, 68
CARREY	12, 21, 78, 71	CASCALLION	56
CARRIE	3, 21, 49, 68, 87	CASE	68
CARRINGTON	8, 87	CASEY	1, 11, 49
CARRIOCK	67	CASIN	21
CARROCH	3	CASS	68
CARROCHAN	49, 89	CASSADY	20, 23, 89
CARROL	26, 37, 71, 87	CASSE	68
CARROLL	28, 37, 50, 87	CASSELLS	23, 33, 37
CARRON	JACOBITE, CARLISLE, 1747, AM	CASSIDY	23, 37, 50
		CASSIE	1, 11, 68
CARRUBER	62	CASSILLS	8, 38, 50
CARRUTH	21, 37, 71	CASSILS	20, 37, 50
CARRY	1, 23, 47, 68, 87	CASSY	8, 12, 28, 71
CARS	67	CASTEEN	36
CARSCADDAN	35	CASTEL	1, 11
CARSE	26, 28, 56, 67	CASTEL	11
CARSEL	33, 71	CASTELAW	36
CARSEWELL	5, 21, 56, 71	CASTELLAW	36
CARSLAW	36, 37, 50, 71	CASTELLO	20, 36
CARSLILE	8, 21, 49	CASTELLOE	36
CARSS	12, 26, 28	CASTELLOW	36
CARSTON	37, 50	CASTLE	1, 14, 28
CARSWELL	14, 49, 56, 71, 75	CASTLELAW	36
CARTE	67	CASTLELLAW	36
CARTIE	1, 37, 50	CASTRAL	44
CARTIN	8	CASTRALL	44
CARTLIDGE	26	CASY	8
CARTNAY	36	CATANACH	1, 3
CARTNEY	36	CATENACH	3, 47, 67
CARTON	37, 50, 67	CATHAN	87
CARTY	3, 23, 88	CATHEL	28, 56, 67
CARUS	JACOBITE, PRESTON, 1716, AM	CATHELS	67
		CATHELS	3, 23
CARVEL	3	CATHER	26, 50, 67, 83

SURNAME	DISTRICT	SURNAME	DISTRICT
CATHERWOOD	8, 70, 71, 83	CHAPMAN	3, 47, 48, 88
CATHIN	87	CHAPPEL	1, 37, 47
CATHLES	67	CHARLESTON	28, 50, 89
CATHRAE	75	CHARLETON	20, 67, 75
CATHRO	3, 23, 33	CHARLTON	21, 50, 88
CATION	33, 48, 67	CHASSAR	3, 23, 47
CATLEE	87	CHASSELS	37, 50
CATLIE	87	CHATTIE	28, 56, 88
CATLY	87	CHATTO	75
CATON	23, 67, 88	CHAVERS	1
CATTANOCH	28, 56, 58	CHAVIS	1
CATTENACH	3, 67, 75	CHAVOUS	1
CATTERSON	53	CHEAP	23, 26, 33, 67
CATTO	1, 10, 47	CHEAPE	14, 33, 67
CATTONACH	1	CHEEVERS	1
CAUFIELD	5, 37, 89	CHEIN	47
CAUGHEY	37, 71, 89	CHESNEY	21, 49, 89
CAULFIELD	36	CHESSAR	1, 47
CAULL	11, 20, 58	CHESSER	1, 47
CAUTION	1, 3, 33	CHIESLEY	87
CAVANAGH	28, 56, 87, 89	CHILDRESS	36
CAVANAH	28, 37, 50	CHIRNSIDE	12, 26, 22, 75, 87
CAVEN	21, 36, 89	CHISHOLM	12, 45, 75
CAVENAH	37	CHISHOLME	28, 75, 77
CAVENS	36	CHIVAS	1, 47
CAVERHILL	87	CHIVES	1
CAVERTON	75	CHOMAR	50
CAVET	49	CHOSEWOOD	26
CAVIE	86	CHREE	1, 11
CAVIN	21, 49, 89	CHRICHTON	17, 37, 48, 50, 87
CAWSON	JACOBITE, 1716, AM	CHRICTON	37, 50, 89
CELLARS	33, 37, 50	CHRIGHTON	1, 33, 67
CELLEM	77	CHRISTAL	1, 49, 67
CENTRE	1, 11, 23	CHRISTIESON	3
CHADWICK	28, 56, 75	CHRON	21
CHAMBERLAIN	1, 28, 56, 87	CHRYSTALL	23, 47, 89
CHAMPNESS	37	CHRYSTIE	1, 5, 67
CHANDLER	1, 26, 37	CHURCH	21, 67, 75
CHAPEL	3, 14, 23, 56	CHYNE	2, 89
CHAPLAIN	1, 3, 23, 37	CLACHER	8, 37, 49, 89
CHAPLIN	3, 20, 23	CLACKSON	37

SURNAME	DISTRICT	SURNAME	DISTRICT
CLAMP	36	CLINKSCALE	1, 12, 75, 87
CLANAGHAN	49	CLINKSCALES	87
CLANCY	45, 50, 71	CLINKSKILL	87
CLANNIE	8	CLINKSKILLS	87
CLANNY	8	CLINT	21, 49, 89
CLAPERTON	12, 26, 28	CLINTON	36, 49, 50, 71
CLARALEE	75	CLINTS	87
CLARALY	75	CLOGG	23
CLARKIN	37, 50	CLONEY	50
CLARKSIN	56	CLOSE	8, 37, 49
CLARKSTON	20, 37, 50, 89	CLOUDSLEY	3, 23, 37
CLARKSTONE	37	CLOUDSLIE	3
CLASON	50, 56, 89	CLOUDSLY	3
CLASPER	8	CLOUGH	23, 28, 56
CLASS	37, 48, 50	CLOUSTON	1, 14, 15, 67
CLATHAN	89	CLOW	17, 21, 84, 89
CLATT	1	CLOWE	3, 23, 28, 84
CLAVERING	10	CLOWS	8, 70, 89
CLAWSON	67	CLUB	1, 11
CLAYHILLS	23	CLUBB	1, 11, 37
CLAYPOLE	36	CLUBBS	37, 50
CLAYPOOL	36	CLUCKIE	36
CLAYTON	11, 17, 58	CLUFF	1
CLAZY	12, 28, 75	CLUGSTONE	36
CLEGHORN	12, 67, 77	CLUNAR	45, 75
CLEMENTS	49, 71, 89	CLUNAS	63, 75, 89
CLEMISON	87	CLUNG	36
CLEMMER	36	CLUNIS	1, 28, 45
CLEMONT	49, 67, 89	CLUTTON	86
CLENHILL	87	CLYDE	3, 23, 83, 88
CLEPHEN	35	CLYDESDALE	37, 48, 50, 83
CLERCHEW	1	COALEY	1
CLERIHEW	1	COALSTONE	26
CLERIHEWS	1	COATNEY	37
CLEUGH	12, 23, 75, 86	COBAN	1, 58, 67
CLEW	37, 50	COBBAIN	1
CLEZY	28, 77, 88	COBBAN	1, 2, 17, 58
CLIFF	44	COBBLER	87
CLIFFORD	20, 37, 50	COBBS	37, 50
CLINGAN	8, 21, 49	COBIN	JACOBITE, 1716, AM
CLINK	48, 67, 69	COBLER	87

SURNAME	DISTRICT	SURNAME	DISTRICT
COCKAYNE	37	COLQUHOUNE	5, 45
COCKER	1, 47, 87	COLSPY	86
COCKERHAM	87	COLSTON	26, 28, 56
COCKFIELD	26, 37, 50	COLSTONE	56
COCKHILL	44	COLT	67
COCKIE	1, 3, 47	COLTARD	49, 77
COCKILL	44	COLTART	21, 36, 71
COCKING	67	COLTHART	21, 37, 50
COCKINGS	67	COLTHEAD	87
COCKS	23	COLTHERD	12, 26, 67, 77
COCKTRIE	36	COLTHERED	87
COCKY	1	COLTHERS	36
CODY	8, 71	COLTON	87
COE	62	COLTRAN	36
COGAN	15, 37, 50, 87	COMBS	20, 33, 49
COGGAN	87	COMBY	DUNBAR, 1650, AM
COGHAL	15	COMMELIN	49
COGHIL	15	COMOLQUOY	15
COKE	50, 63, 67	CONAGHAN	37, 50
COLBERT	1, 89	CONAHER	JACOBITE, PRESTON,
COLDEN	87		1716, AM
COLDINHAM	87	CONALLY	3, 23, 88
COLDSTREAM	28, 56, 87, 89	CONAN	3, 15, 23, 39, 87
COLDWELLS	26, 56	CONCHAR	28, 49, 56
COLEY	1, 3, 23	CONCHIE	21, 49, 89
COLFORD	37	CONES	1
COLGAN	5, 37, 50	CONESON	39
COLISON	28, 56, 67	CONGHAL	84
COLLANS	37, 50, 89	CONGLE	84
COLLEDGE	20, 58, 75	CONHEATH	36
COLLEN	12, 20, 89	CONING	36
COLLER	1, 23, 33	CONLAN	23, 37, 50
COLLEY	1, 28, 37, 50	CONLEY	3, 23, 37
COLLIE	1, 47, 50	CONLIN	12, 21, 89
COLLIESON	1, 3	CONNACHER	33, 67, 86
COLLIGAN	23	CONNAL	20, 49, 89
COLLIN	12, 33, 67	CONNALL	28, 49, 67
COLLINS	3, 17, 37, 67, 82	CONNAN	1, 42, 39, 87, 88
COLLISON	1, 47, 56	CONNAR	1, 26, 37, 60
COLLY	1, 45	CONNEL	8, 14, 49
COLON	28, 56, 75	CONNELLY	14, 20, 37

SURNAME	DISTRICT	SURNAME	DISTRICT
CONNER	20, 23, 50, 60, 71	COPLEY	37, 50, 71
CONNERS	20	COPPACH	52
CONNING	36, 49, 67, 89	COPPLEY	37
CONNLEY	5, 37, 48	COPPOCH	52
CONNOL	28, 56, 67	CORBERT	75
CONNOLEY	37	CORBRIDGE	75
CONNOLY	50	CORDINER	1, 28
CONNORS	28, 37, 56	CORDWAINER	1
CONNOWAY	37, 50, 71	CORDWAYNER	1
CONOCHER	67	CORE	20, 50, 67, 83
CONOLLY	23, 47, 49	CORELY	37
CONOLOY	71	COREY	36
CONON	1, 67	CORHEAD	36
CONOW	JACOBITE, PRESTON, 1716, AM	CORK	28, 47, 56, 83
		CORKRAN	36
CONQUER	26, 37	CORKRANE	36
CONQUERGOOD	28, 56	CORMIC	56
CONQUET	56	CORMIE	33, 58, 60, 71
CONSE	68	CORNACK	36
CONSON	39	CORNAK	36
CONSTANTINE	83	CORNAL	3, 8, 67
CONVALL	83	CORNE	26, 37, 50
CONVELL	83	CORNELL	87
CONVERY	50	CORNET	26, 28, 37, 56
CONVEY	50	CORNEULL	83
CONWAY	23, 28, 37, 50	CORNFOOT	3, 20, 23, 33
COOCK	3, 28, 56	CORNS	20, 28, 50
COOIL	37	CORNTON	89
COOKE	3, 14, 20	CORNWALL	1, 26, 56, 89
COOMBS	DUNBAR, 1650, AM	CORNWALLE	89
COOPAR	3, 23, 75	CORPHINSTONE	87
COOPLAND	71	CORRIE	11, 21, 49
COOSAR	87	CORRIGAL	67
COOSER	87	CORRIGAN	20, 37, 50
COOTE	50	CORRIGILL	67
COPACH	52	CORRY	36
COPACK	52	CORSAN	8, 21, 36
COPELAND	21, 36, 47, 49, 87	CORSANE	36
COPELY	37	CORSAR	89
COPLAND	36, 49, 67, 89	CORSBIE	12, 26, 49, 60
COPLAY	37	CORSBY	12

SURNAME	DISTRICT	SURNAME	DISTRICT
CORSCADDAN	35	COULLIE	3, 21, 47
CORSE	3, 28, 56, 67	COULTARD	21, 49
CORSECADDON	35	COULTART	21, 33, 49
CORSEHILL	1	COULTER	8, 36, 37, 89
CORSER	89	COULTHARD	8, 21, 36
CORSIE	67	COULTHART	21, 28, 56
CORSKIE	1	COUPLAND	21, 49, 89
CORSKY	1	COURAGE	2
CORSON	21, 36, 49, 75	COURNEY	56
CORSSAR	89	COURT	28, 67, 89
CORSTON	28, 56, 67, 69	COURTENAY	8, 37, 50
CORSTONE	67	COURTNEY	22
COSALT	44	COUSAR	87
COSBIE	89	COUSER	8, 20, 87, 89
COSENS	3, 12, 23	COUSIN	48, 63, 77
COSKIER	36	COUSINS	1, 71, 89
COSKRIE	89	COUSTIN	28, 33, 56
COSKRY	28, 49, 56	COUSTON	3
COSSANS	3, 23	COUT	67, 69, 89
COSSAR	12, 56, 60, 67, 87	COUTE	1, 3
COSSER	12, 56, 58	COUTLS	56
COSSIE	21	COUTT	17, 33, 89
COSTA	67	COUTTIE	3, 23, 67
COSTERMAN	87	COUTTY	3
COSTIN	36	COUTY	3
COSTINE	21, 49	COVENTRY	17, 33, 48, 87
COTHART	5	COVEY	37, 50
COTHILL	3, 26, 67	COVINGTON	83
COTHRELL	23	COW	1, 12, 26, 30, 62
COTHRILL	23	COWBROUGH	5, 71, 89
COTTINGHAM	47	COWDEN	26, 49, 89
COTTRAM	87	COWE	11, 12, 26, 30, 62
COTTRELL	80	COWGILL	83
COTTS	1, 21, 36	COWIESON	1, 11, 47
COUBRO	1	COWLEY	3, 20, 23
COUBROUGH	1, 37, 50, 89	COWLIE	3, 23, 28
COUCHER	21	COWNIE	3, 67, 89
COUDIE	33, 49, 50	COWRAGE	2
COUGHAN	50	COWRIE	5, 67, 89
COUGHLIN	37, 50	COWSER	88
COUGHTRIE	8, 49, 89	COWSON	JACOBITE, 1716, AM

SURNAME	DISTRICT	SURNAME	DISTRICT
COWT	87	CRAIR	1, 89
COWTIE	JACOBITE, 1716, AM	CRAISE	12, 26, 56
COX	5, 8, 28, 89	CRAITH	8, 37, 49
COXE	5	CRAKE	21, 26
COYNE	3, 21, 23	CRAMMMOND	87
CRAB	3, 23, 47	CRAMMOND	3, 23, 75
CRABB	1, 3, 23, 47, 60	CRAMMUND	87
CRABBE	1, 23, 28, 56, 60	CRAMON	28, 37, 56
CRACHET	3	CRAMOND	3, 23, 75, 87
CRACHETT	3	CRAMONG	67
CRADDOCK	28, 33, 56	CRAMONT	75, 77
CRAELL	23	CRAMPTON	56, 67
CRAGEN	1, 67	CRAMUND	87
CRAGGIE	1, 67	CRAN	1, 3, 11, 12
CRAGON	85	CRANDAL	83
CRAIB	1, 11, 44	CRANDALIE	83
CRAICK	3, 12, 67	CRANDALL	83
CRAIGAILLIE	67	CRANDALLIE	83
CRAIGAILLY	67	CRANE	1, 3, 26
CRAIGALLIE	67	CRANMER	20, 37, 67
CRAIGALLY	67	CRANN	3, 37, 50, 88
CRAIGAN	1, 11, 28, 44, 86	CRANNA	3
CRAIGEN	1, 11, 44, 67, 95	CRANSTONE	12, 50, 75
CRAIGFORTH	89	CRASTER	37
CRAIGHEAD	1, 8, 23	CRAVEN	21, 26, 47, 36
CRAIGHILL	67	CRAVENS	21, 36, 49
CRAIGIE	8, 15, 33, 60, 67, 69	CRAW	11, 12, 56, 87
CRAIGIN	87	CRAWFURD	12, 71, 75
CRAIGMILE	1, 47	CREAM	50
CRAIGMILLER	87	CREANER	3
CRAIGMYLE	1, 47	CREAR	15, 48, 67
CRAIGNICH	5	CREASE	12, 28, 56, 60
CRAIGNISH	5	CREDIE	21, 36, 49, 89
CRAIGON	1, 3, 23	CREELMAN	8, 28, 37, 56
CRAIGOW	68	CREELY	8
CRAIGS	12, 33, 37	CREEVIE	1
CRAIGTON	3	CREEVY	1
CRAIGY	8, 15	CREICHTON	21, 50
CRAIK	12, 36, 49, 67	CREMON	44
CRAIN	3	CRENNA	3
CRAINE	3	CRERAG	89

SURNAME	DISTRICT	SURNAME	DISTRICT
CRESSWEL	JACOBITE, 1716, AM	CROKATT	77, 86, 89
CRESSWELL	JACOBITE, 1716, AM	CROLE	67
CREVIE	1	CROLEY	26, 28, 56
CREVY	1	CROLL	1, 3, 23, 47
CREWER	67	CROLLA	36
CRIBB	83, 87	CROLLAGH	36
CRIBBES	83, 87	CROM	3, 50, 67
CRIBBIS	12, 56	CROMDALE	85
CRIBBS	83, 87	CRON	3, 5, 21, 26
CRICHTOUN	COVENANTER, 1684, AM	CRONE	5, 21, 49, 89
CRICK	11	CROOK	3, 68, 81, 89
CRIEFF	55	CROOKE	68
CRIERIE	49	CROOKES	68
CRIEVE	55	CROOKS	12, 26, 48
CRIGHALL	87	CROOKSHANK	1, 11, 67
CRIGHTON	67	CROOKSHANKS	1, 58, 71
CRILEY	33	CROOKSTON	33, 50, 56
CRILLY	20, 50, 89	CROOME	ROYALIST, 1652, AM
CRILY	33	CROSAN	50
CRINAN	67	CROSER	37, 50, 75
CRINGLE	68	CROSSHILL	83
CRINKLEY	75	CROSSHONE	44
CRIPPLE	67	CROSSLEY	15
CRIRIE	21, 49	CROSSTHWAITE	50
CRITCHLIE	44	CROSSWAITE	23
CRITCHLY	44	CROSSWHITE	23
CROAL	3, 28, 47	CROSTIE	36
CROALL	3, 23, 28, 47	CROSTY	36
CROCHAT	3, 36, 83	CROUCH	28, 44, 56
CROCHATT	3, 36, 83	CROUCHER	75
CROCHET	3, 36, 83	CROUNER	1
CROCHETT	3, 36, 83	CROWHART	87
CROCKART	3, 23, 67	CROWHEART	87
CROCKAT	3, 67, 88	CROWLEY	37, 50, 75
CROCKERT	1, 67	CROZER	8, 12, 75, 77, 89
CROCKET	21, 47, 49	CRUCKSHANK	1, 9, 11, 58
CROCKFORD	ROYALIST, 1651, AM	CRUICKSHANKS	1, 3, 23, 58
CROFT	JACOBITE, 1716, AM	CRUIKSHANK	1, 11, 58
CROGAN	5	CRUIKSHANKS	15, 58, 88
CROGGAN	5	CRUIZANE	87
CROHAM	67	CRUIZEAN	87

SURNAME	DISTRICT	SURNAME	DISTRICT
CRUME	87	CUPPLE	53
CRUMME	87	CUPPLES	53, 60
CRUNKLETON	75	CURE	8, 70, 88
CRUSCADDAN	35	CURL	12, 14, 21, 68
CRUSCADDEN	35	CURLE	12, 14, 75
CRUZANE	87	CURLET	8, 89
CRUZEAN	87	CURLL	28, 56, 86
CRYBBACE	28, 56	CURMUCKHELL	WORCESTER, 1652, AM
CRYING	1	CURRAN	8, 15, 49, 89
CUBBIE	3	CURRANCE	23, 49, 89
CUBBISON	36	CURRANS	37, 71, 89
CUBBISTON	36	CURREN	8
CUBBY	3	CURRER	22, 28, 33, 67
CUBIE	3, 8, 50, 89	CURROR	22, 28, 33, 48
CUBISON	36	CURSATTER	67
CUBISTON	36	CURTIS	3
CUBY	3	CURWENS	75
CUDDIE	20, 36, 88, 89	CURWINS	75
CUDDY	8, 36, 50, 89	CURZON	36
CUGAN	3, 23, 71	CUSAR	87
CULBERSON	50, 67, 75	CUSER	87
CULBERT	3, 17, 33, 67	CUSHEY	75
CULBERTSON	17, 67, 75, 87	CUSHIE	33, 75
CULLENS	26, 67, 89	CUSHNIE	1, 44, 47
CULLEY	8, 12, 37	CUSHNY	44
CULLISH	36	CUSHY	33
CULLISON	1	CUSSAR	87
CULLTON	49	CUSSER	87
CULLY	23, 50, 89	CUTCHEON	49, 89
CULOMB	36	CUTELAR	36
CULP	1	CUTELER	36
CULTON	21, 28, 36	CUTELLAR	36
CUMING	1, 23, 28, 56	CUTELLER	36
CUMLAQUOY	15, 71	CUTHBERT	3, 48, 63
CUMMERS	2	CUTHBERTS	3, 11
CUMNOCK	68	CUTHBERTSON	3, 8, 67, 77
CUMRAY	84	CUTHELL	62
CUNACH	2	CUTHIL	48, 77, 88
CUNDIE	44	CUTHILL	3, 12, 23, 30, 62
CUNNEN	36	CUTLER	22
CUNNING	11, 28, 33, 36, 60	CUTT	67

SURNAME	DISTRICT	SURNAME	DISTRICT
CUTTLER	22	DALL	3, 17, 33
CYHNE	1	DALLING	21, 36, 49, 50, 87
CYNOCH	1	DALLY	36, 49, 81, 89
DABSON	35	DALSIEL	50
DABZIELL	50	DALTON	1, 36, 50
DACKAR	1, 75	DALWHINNIE	52
DACKER	1, 75	DALWHINNY	52
DACRE	1, 75	DALY	23, 28, 56
DACRES	3, 28, 47	DAMON	3, 23
DAER	3, 23	DAND	3, 23
DAES	23, 28, 88	DANDIE	3, 23, 33
DAFFAN	83	DANDISON	36
DAFFEN	83	DANDY	3, 23, 37
DAFFRON	28, 56	DANES	50
DAG	1, 54	DANIELS	DUNBAR, 1650, AM
DAGG	1, 54	DANIELSON	17, 23, 33, 50, 89
DAGGS	1, 54	D'ANNAN	67
DAGS	1, 54	D'ANNAND	67
DAICK	37, 50	DANSKIN	20, 23, 33, 89
DAIDLE	87	DANSKINE	28, 67, 89
DAILLY	71, 88, 89	DANSON	75
DAILY	37, 50, 89	DARBY	1, 8, 20, 88
DAINTY	83	DARGAVEL	21, 49, 88
DAIRES	26, 50	DARGAVELL	68
DAIRY	8, 37, 50	DARGIE	3, 23, 67, 87
DAISLEY	50	DARGO	1
DAKERS	3, 23, 47	DARGS	62
DALBECK	75	DARGUE	28, 56
DALBY	37, 50	DARGY	3, 87
DALCILLE	44	DARLEITH	83
DALCROSS	68	DARLEY	36
DALE	1, 8, 26, 88	DARLING	12, 26, 60, 75, 87
DALES	8, 37, 50	DARNICK	75
DALGARNO	1, 11, 67	DARNLY	56
DALGETY	3, 23, 89	DARREL	87
DALGINCH	22	DARRELL	87
DALGITY	3, 23, 89	DARRIE	12, 26, 33, 75
DALGLEISH	67, 75, 77	DARRY	75
DALGLIESH	21, 31, 33, 67, 77	DARSEY	33
DALGLISH	67, 77, 89	DASHER	53
DALHAM	36	DASPHER	53

SURNAME	DISTRICT	SURNAME	DISTRICT
DASS	15	DENGELL	WORCESTER, 1652, AM
DASSANVILLE	28, 56	DENGLE	WORCESTER, 1652, AM
DASSON	35	DENHAM	12, 17, 26, 60
DAUGALL	89	DENHOLM	12, 26, 56, 75
DAUN	11, 20, 47	DENHOLME	28, 56, 75
DAVENIE	1	DENIVAN	89
DAVENPORT	21, 28, 56	DENMARK	8, 37, 50
DAVENTRIE	87	DENNAN	8, 37, 50
DAVENTRY	87	DENNET	17, 28, 56
DAVENY	1	DENNETT	28, 56, 60
DAVIES	2, 21, 48, 49, 50, 89	DENNEY	50
DAVNIE	1	DENNING	84
DAWES	3, 23, 45	DENNY	19, 20, 37, 50, 71
DAWKINS	87	DENNYS	19
DAYER	20, 23, 75	DENOVAN	17, 28, 89
DAZLEY	50	DENOVIN	89
DE QUENCY	8, 33	DENSON	36
DEACON	8, 23, 44, 48	DENT	33, 48, 50
DEAKIN	44	DERAND	15
DEALLY	33, 50, 88	DERBIE	8
DEANS	2, 12, 26, 50, 75	DERBY	14, 21, 49
DEAR	3, 23, 47	DERDEN	75
DEARNESS	15, 28, 56, 67	DERMONT	8, 21, 71
DEARRIE	8	DERNESS	67
DEARY	21, 37, 50, 71	DERRIN	28, 56
DEAVIS	50	DERRITT	JACOBITE, 1716, AM
DEER	1, 28, 56	DESKIE	85
DEERAN	15	DESKIEK	85
DEERE	1	DESKIEKEY	85
DEES	8, 33	DESKIEKY	85
DEGNAN	37, 50	DESLEY	56
DEIGHTON	28, 56, 67	DEUCHARS	3, 23, 67
DELANY	50, 71, 75	DEUCHRASS	37, 50
DELDAY	28, 56, 67	DEVAN	50
DELL	ROYALIST, 1651, AM	DEVANEY	37, 50
DEMAR	37	DEVANIE	23
DEMPESTER	8	DEVANY	23
DEMPSEY	3, 23, 37, 67	DEVELIN	37, 50, 88
DEMPSIE	67	DEVELINE	3, 23, 71
DEMPSTER	8, 17, 48, 49, 84	DEVEN	8
DEN	2	DEVILIN	3, 21, 23

SURNAME	DISTRICT	SURNAME	DISTRICT
DEVINE	1, 23, 37, 50	DINNIESTON	21
DEVIT	37, 50, 71	DINNING	8, 20, 84, 71
DEVLIN	23, 37, 50	DINNINGS	84
DEVON	28, 71, 89	DINNON	37, 50, 89
DEWARS	3, 23, 67	DINNY	1, 3, 37, 54, 71
DEWHURST	28, 56	DINON	5, 8, 71
DIACK	1, 23, 37, 50	DIPPIE	87
DIAMOND	3, 37, 49, 50, 89	DIPPLE	12, 28, 44, 75
DIAMONT	3	DIPPY	87
DICKE	1, 17	DIRLAND	75
DICKENSON	JACOBITE, PRESTON, 1716, AM	DIRLETON	87
		DISHER	28, 33, 37
DICKER	8, 17, 33, 50	DISHINGTON	26, 33, 75
DICKERS	85	DITCHBURN	33
DICKETT	67	DIVENTRE	68
DICKIE	1, 8, 17	DIVERTIE	1, 47
DICKIESON	50, 71, 75	DIVERTY	1
DICKINSON	12, 68, 75, 77	DIVINE	1, 20, 37, 50
DICKMAN	28, 56, 75	DIVINY	1
DICKS	28	DOCHARD	5, 67, 89
DICUS	83	DOCHARTY	14, 37, 50, 71
DIESKEY	85	DOCKAR	11
DIESKY	85	DOCTOR	3, 23, 36, 67
DIGGINS	8, 37, 50	DODGSON	3
DIGNAN	44	DODS	12, 67, 75
DIKE	85	DOE	67
DIKER	85	DOEG	8, 33, 67
DIKES	85	DOEY	71
DILL	26, 36, 44 49, 89	DOGAN	37, 50
DILLIDA	1	DOGHERTY	50
DILLIDAFF	1	DOHERTY	20, 37, 71
DILLON	3, 23, 37	DOLAN	28, 49, 56
DIMMA	56, 75, 88	DOLEPAIN	36
DIMMER	52	DOLFIN	75
DIN	87	DOLFINESTON	75
DINGALL	3, 67, 69	DOLFINESTONE	75
DINGWELL	58, 67, 75	DOLLAN	8, 23, 28, 89
DINN	87	DOLLANLEN	23
DINNEL	36	DOLLAR	17, 20, 47, 89
DINNET	67	DOLLARD	44
DINNIE	1, 54, 12, 47	DONAGAN	28, 50, 56

SURNAME	DISTRICT	SURNAME	DISTRICT
DONAGHIE	8, 37, 50	DORREN	36
DONALLY	8, 28, 56	DORTHAN	3
DONAT	3, 26, 33, 84	DORTHON	3
DONATT	84	DORWOOD	1, 3, 23
DONDALE	54	DOT	56
DONEGAN	28, 37, 50	DOUCHALL	68
DONELLY	37, 50, 71	DOUGALD	71, 88, 89
DONELSON	67	DOUGAN	8, 36, 37, 89
DONET	23, 33, 48	DOUGGAN	89
DONN	15, 47, 54, 67	DOUGHAN	36
DONNACHIE	50	DOUGHARTY	8, 50, 71
DONNACLIRE	8	DOUGHERTY	20, 21, 37, 50
DONNALLY	20, 37, 89	DOUGHTIE	20, 28, 37, 75
DONNAN	8, 36, 49, 89	DOUGHTY	17, 26, 30, 62, 89
DONNAT	3, 23, 67	DOUGLASS	47, 67, 75
DONNE	21, 28, 88	DOUL	11, 15, 89
DONNELLY	37, 50, 71	DOULE	20, 28, 56
DONNET	3, 23, 28	DOUN	15, 63, 88
DONNOCHIE	8, 37, 50	DOUNAN	5, 89
DONNOCHY	8	DOUNES	12
DONNOLLY	28, 50, 56	DOUNIE	8, 15, 21
DONOGHUE	28, 56	DOUNS	20, 81, 89
DOOLAN	20, 37, 50	DOUROCH	71
DOORS	67	DOVERTIE	1
DORAN	26, 36, 71, 89	DOVERTY	1
DORAT	54	DOWAR	1, 33, 67
DORATT	54	DOWD	37, 50, 71
DORIAN	36	DOWDS	8
DORMAN	8, 23, 49, 89	DOWER	1, 47, 56
DORMAND	89	DOWN	8, 50, 75
DORMANT	37, 50	DOWNING	DUNBAR, 1650, AM
DORMON	89	DOWNS	20, 50, 88
DORNACH	44	DOWTY	DUNBAR, 1650, AM
DORNAN	8, 49, 71	DRAINER	21, 37, 50
DORNEN	21	DRAINIE	44, 58
DORNIE	1	DRAINY	44
DORNOCH	44	DRAKE	85
DORNOK	44	DRAPE	36
DORNY	1	DRAPER	67, 71, 89
DORRANS	71	DRAPPO	37
DORRAT	23, 33, 56	DRAUGHILL	75

SURNAME	DISTRICT	SURNAME	DISTRICT
DRAVER	1, 23, 67	DUESBURY	20
DREDAN	36	DUFFAY	8, 50, 56
DREDEN	36	DUFFES	1, 11, 58
DREDIN	36	DUFFIE	21
DREGHORN	8, 37, 71, 78	DUFFIN	28, 56, 71
DREW	37, 50, 89	DUGAID	1
DREWETT	3, 67	DUGAN	20, 36, 49, 89
DREWITT	3	DUGETT	1
DRIDAN	3	DUGGAN	36, 37, 49, 50, 56
DRIDEN	3	DUGGIE	44
DRIMMIE	3, 47, 67	DUGGY	44
DRIMMY	67	DUGID	1
DRIPP	83	DUGITT	1
DRIPPS	83	DUGLAD	58
DRON	3, 33, 67	DUGLES	DUNBAR, 1650, AM
DRONE	37, 50, 67	DUGUID	1, 47
DROVER	28, 50, 56, 88	DUIRS	3, 47, 67
DRUM	1, 33, 67	DUKE	1, 3, 23, 49
DRUMBECK	1	DUKIE	8, 17
DRUMBRECK	67	DULEN	WORCESTER, 1652, AM
DRUMM	1, 33	DULLEHANLY	36
DRUMMON	71	DULLEN	44
DRYBOROUGH	28, 33, 56	DULLIN	44
DRYBOURGH	75	DULLY	44
DRYBURGH	28, 33, 56, 75	DULTON	8, 37, 50
DRYBURN	87	DULY	3
DRYBURNE	87	DUMBAR	8, 47, 71
DRYDON	49, 75, 77	DUMBARTON	19, 83
DRYLAW	87	DUMBER	3, 89
DRYLIE	83	DUMBRECK	28, 56, 88
DRYLY	83	DUMBRETTON	83
DRYNAN	8, 71, 89	DUMFREYS	36
DRYSDALL	26, 48, 89	DUMFRIES	36
DRYSDEN	3	DUNBARNEY	84
DUBUCAN	3	DUNBARNY	84
DUCAT	1, 23, 28, 56	DUNBARTON	83
DUCATT	1	DUNBLANE	87
DUDDINGSTON	87	DUNCALL	36
DUDDINGTON	87	DUNCOLL	36
DUDGEON	26, 30, 62, 75, 77	DUNDEE	23
DUDSON	21	DUNFEE	44

SURNAME	DISTRICT	SURNAME	DISTRICT
DUNFIE	44	DURNIN	37, 50, 89
DUNFIES	44	DURNO	1, 12
DUNGALSON	83	DURRANDS	15, 22
DUNGAVEL	50	DURRANT	2
DUNGAVELL	56, 88	DURRAR	1
DUNIPACE	37, 50, 88, 89	DURREY	3, 23
DUNKELD	21, 28, 49, 67	DUSKY	15
DUNLAVIE	37, 81, 89	DUSTAN	1, 11, 58
DUNLEARY	20	DUSTIE	67
DUNLOOP	8	DUSTY	67
DUNMORE	8, 88, 89	DUTCH	23, 33, 47, 67
DUNNE	1, 3, 44, 50	DUTHIL	85
DUNNELY	44	DUTHILL	85
DUNNIGAN	37, 50	DUTT	8
DUNNING	8, 20, 28, 84	DUTTON	8, 37, 50
DUNOON	1, 15	DUYS	45
DUNOVAN	89	DWYER	20, 28, 37
DUNOVEN	89	DYACK	1
DUNPHIE	44	DYALL	71
DUNPHY	44	DYAT	30
DUNS	12, 28, 56, 87	DYATT	30
DUNSCORE	36	DYCUS	83
DUNSE	12, 28, 87, 89	DYKAR	85
DUNSHIE	36	DYKARS	85
DUNSHIRE	83	DYKE	85
DUNSHY	36	DYKER	85
DUNSIRE	83	DYKERS	85
DUNSMUIR	8, 50	DYKES	8, 50, 67, 85
DUNSMUIT	37	DYMOCK	14, 67, 88
DUNSMURE	8, 17, 28	EADAILE	83
DUNWOODIE	12, 21, 75	EAGAN	45
DURAND	22	EAGER	DUNBAR, 1650, AM
DURANT	1	EAGLESFIELD	36
DURAY	3	EAGLESHAM	8, 68, 71, 89
DURDLE	44	EAGLESOM	71
DURES	37, 50	EAGLESOME	53
DURHAM	28, 47, 75, 89	EARL	8, 37, 50, 78, 71
DURKIE	3, 23, 33	EARLE	68
DURLAND	75	EARLSON	87
DURNEY	1	EARLSTON	37
DURNIE	1	EARLY	20, 37, 49

SURNAME	DISTRICT	SURNAME	DISTRICT
EARSMAN	21, 28, 56	EDWARD	3, 47, 58, 83
EASDALE	8, 37, 50, 83	EDWARDS	1, 11, 83
EASDON	8, 17, 71	EDWARDSON	83
EASIE	3	EDWART	75
EASSIE	3	EFFINGHAM	28, 56
EASTMEAD	44	EGAN	20, 37, 49
EASTON	21, 50, 56, 75, 87, 88	EGGOE	JACOBITE, 1716, AM
EASTWOOD	68	EGLESHAM	8
EATTEN	47	EGLINGBURG	30
EAVES	56	EGLINTON	30, 20, 50, 71
EBAUGH	1	EGO	1, 54, 3, 11
EBBOT	23	EILERTON	86
EBBOTT	23	EILERTSON	86
ECCLES	8, 71, 89	ELDRED	75
ECHLIN	87	ELEALD	87
ECHLINE	87	ELFORD	1
ECKFORD	56, 67, 75	ELGE	23
ECKLAND	3, 23, 89	ELGEY	23
ECKLES	50, 87	ELGIN	1, 28, 56, 85
ECLES	28, 56	ELIRICK	2
EDDINGTON	23, 28, 56	ELISON	56, 75
EDDISLAW	87	ELL	36
EDDISON	1, 11, 47	ELLEM	87
EDGLAS	87	ELLEN	44, 87
EDGLEY	12, 28, 56, 87	ELLERMAN	44
EDINBORO	87	ELLESLEY	84
EDINBURGH	87	ELLICE	23, 48, 63
EDINSTON	12, 26, 75, 87	ELLINGHAM	7
EDINSTONE	87	ELLON	1
EDMINSHIRE	87	ELLRICK	1
EDMINSTONE	WORCESTER, 1652, AM	ELLUM	87
EDMINSTREIRE	WORCESTER, 1652, AM	ELMER	23, 26
EDMOND	1, 26, 89	ELMSLEY	12, 28, 56
EDMONDS	28, 56, 75	ELMSLIE	1, 47, 88
EDMONDSTON	83, 75, 88, 89	ELMSLY	1
EDMONDSTONE	83	ELPHINSTON	1, 87
EDMONSTON	26, 28, 56	ELRICK	1, 11
EDMUND	1, 28, 56, 89	ELSMIE	1
EDMUNDS	28, 56, 71	ELSTON	75
EDNAM	75	ELTON	1, 20, 21
EDNEY	33, 56	ELVIN	21, 50, 71

SURNAME	DISTRICT	SURNAME	DISTRICT
ELWIS	63	ESSY	3
ELWISE	63	ESTBRIDGE	44
ELYER	DUNBAR, 1650, AM	ESTON	3, 71, 89
EMAN	12, 67	ESTRIDGE	44
EMBERSON	8	ETBORN	87
EMERY	DUNBAR, 1650, AM	ETBORNE	87
EMLAY	26, 56	ETHERINGTON	3, 28, 56
EMM	36	ETTERSHANK	1, 47
EMOLIE	56	ETTLES	11, 45, 58
EMOND	12, 75, 77	EVANS	12, 20, 28, 50
EMSLEY	28, 58, 88	EVERETT	1, 3, 37
EMSLIE	1, 47, 56	EVERLIE	67
ENGAIN	75	EVERLY	67
ENGAINE	75	EVIOTT	3
ENGLAND	1, 11, 23	EWANS	23, 77, 89
ENGLISH	37, 71, 75, 89	EWANSON	28, 67, 89
ENLOE	87	EWARD	21, 86, 89
ENTREKEN	67	EWART	21, 26, 49
ENTREKIN	67	EWENS	8, 75, 89
ENTRELOTT	67	EWENSON	28, 56, 89
ENVERDALE	67	EWNSON	67, 89
EPPS	53	EYLES	28, 56, 89
ERCILDON	87	EYRE	28, 37, 56, 75
ERCILDOUN	87	EYRES	75
ERD	3	EYTON	47
ERICKSON	28, 33, 56	FAA	87
ERRIDGE	86	FABER	67
ERRITCK	31	FACHNEY	84
ESDAILE	1	FACHNIE	84
ESDAILE	8	FACKNEY	84
ESDION	89	FACKNIE	84
ESDON	71, 89	FADDIE	1, 3
ESDONESDON	20	FADE	12
ESKDALE	21, 67, 75	FAFALGAR	50
ESPIE	17, 71, 89	FAGAN	28, 49, 56
ESPLEY	89	FAH	87
ESPLIE	89	FAHEY	28, 56, 89
ESPLIN	3, 23, 75	FAHS	87
ESPLY	89	FAHY	37, 50
ESSIE	3	FAICHNEY	17, 67, 88
ESSONE	1	FAICHNIE	84

SURNAME	DISTRICT	SURNAME	DISTRICT
FAIN	8	FARGUHARSON	2
FAINE	8	FARIES	21, 89
FAINES	8	FARISH	21, 28, 49
FAINS	8	FARLAN	20, 67, 71
FAIRBURN	8, 12, 75	FARLES	28, 56, 75
FAIRFOWL	33, 47, 56, 88	FARLEY	20, 37, 88
FAIRFUL	3, 23, 33	FARLIE	12, 88, 89
FAIRGRIEVE	67, 75, 77, 87	FARNALL	3
FAIRHAUGH	19	FARNAN	3
FAIRHOLM	83	FARNELL	3
FAIRINGTON	75	FARNEY	67
FAIRM	28, 56, 89	FARNINGTON	12, 75
FAIRNEY	23, 48, 56	FARR	37, 50
FAIRNIE	33, 56, 89	FARRELL	17, 37, 50
FAIRSERVICE	8, 37, 50, 83	FARRIER	1, 47, 49
FAIRWEATHER	3, 23, 47, 67	FARRINGTON	34
FAITCHEN	26	FARRISH	12, 21
FALA	28, 56, 87	FARSBUSH	DUNBAR, 1650, AM
FALAY	36	FASKEN	10
FALCONAR	1, 45, 87	FASKIN	10
FALDS	87	FASLAIN	83
FALKIRK	32	FASLANE	83
FALKNER	23, 28, 56	FASSETT	DUNBAR, 1650, AM
FALKONER	3, 28, 67	FASSINGTON	87
FALLA	28, 75, 77, 87	FASWYDE	87
FALLAS	83	FAUCETT	16
FALLEN	37, 50	FAULD	3, 20, 71
FALLON	11, 50, 67	FAULE	8
FALLOW	12, 50, 75	FAULES	8
FALLS	33, 37, 50, 87	FAUNS	3
FALSIDE	12, 28, 56, 87	FAW	87
FALTON	5	FAWCETT	16
FAMILTON	22, 56	FAWE	87
FANNING	37, 50	FAWES	87
FARBISH	DUNBAR, 1650, AM	FAWNS	3, 23, 47, 87
FARBUSH	DUNBAR, 1650, AM	FAWS	87
FARFOR	3, 67	FAWSIDE	87
FARG	87	FEAD	21, 28, 49
FARGIE	12, 26, 28	FEARGRIEVE	56
FARGISON	DUNBAR, 1650, AM	FEARN	3, 47, 58
FARGUHAR	2	FEARNSIDE	1, 11, 47

SURNAME	DISTRICT	SURNAME	DISTRICT
FECHNEY	50, 67, 71	FIDDLER	1, 67, 75, 83
FECHNIE	84	FIDLER	1, 67, 75
FECHNY	84	FIELDER	56
FEENEY	28, 37, 56, 68	FIELDING	3, 47, 71
FEENIE	68, 89	FIELDS	23, 28, 49
FEGAN	23, 49, 71	FIGGINS	8, 28, 56
FEGUSHILL	8	FILAN	84
FEILDING	3, 50	FILLANS	84
FELIX	37, 50	FILMER	75
FELLOW	8, 85	FILMORE	83
FELLOWES	21, 28, 56, 85	FILP	3
FELLOWS	8, 85	FILSHIE	20, 83
FELSHIE	20	FILSHY	83
FEMISTER	1, 44, 45, 58	FIMISTER	1, 37, 58, 85
FEND	36	FIMMERTON	87
FENDE	36	FINALAYSON	75
FENDER	23, 26, 67, 87	FINCHER	1
FENDIE	87	FINDAL	3, 47
FENDY	87	FINDAY	1, 8, 11
FENNIE	1, 28, 88	FINDEN	54
FENSICK	67	FINDON	54
FERBUSH	DUNBAR, 1650, AM	FINGLAND	21, 28, 49
FERIAR	83	FINGLASS	3
FERLIE	12, 88, 89	FINIGAN	20, 28, 37
FERME	56, 71, 83, 88	FINITER	85
FERMEA	83	FINLATOR	(NFI) 1685, AM
FERMER	3, 23, 37	FINN	3, 23, 50
FERN	37, 50, 86, 89	FINNAN	36
FERNE	37, 50	FINNEGAN	28, 33, 56
FERNS	20, 37, 50	FINNELSTON	8
FERRIAR	83	FINNEN	14, 37
FERRIEF	88	FINNEY	1, 14, 20, 37
FERRIER	3, 33, 44, 47	FINNIE	1, 37, 88
FERRODY	SOLDIER, BANISHED, 1774, AM	FINNIESTON	37
		FINNIGAN	37, 50, 88
FETHERSTON	33	FINNIGHAN	8
FETTES	1, 3, 47	FINNISON	1
FFRESELL	WORCESTER, 1652, AM	FINNY	11, 14, 89
FIDDES	1, 47, 75	FIRSKIN	67
FIDDIS	47, 58, 75	FIRTH	1, 15, 67, 80
FIDDISON	36	FISH	12, 26, 87, 89

SURNAME	DISTRICT	SURNAME	DISTRICT
FISK	33	FLOWERS	12, 23, 49, 77, 87
FISKE	33	FLUGG	44
FISKEN	37, 48, 67, 84	FLYN	37, 71, 89
FISKIN	37, 50, 67, 84	FLYNE	37, 50, 71
FITCHET	3, 23	FLYNN	28, 50, 71, 89
FITCHETT	3, 47	FLYTER	1, 58, 75
FITHIE	3, 23	FOARD	3, 33, 67
FITHY	3	FOGGIE	1, 28, 33, 56
FITSIMONS	71, 81, 89	FOGGO	12, 26, 33, 87
FITZ CHARLES	37, 50	FOGGY	1
FITZ MAURICE	89	FOGO	8, 37, 50
FITZ PATRICK	23, 37, 50	FOLDS	49, 87
FITZ SIMMONS	37, 88, 89	FOLEY	23, 44, 88, 89
FITZ SIMON	8, 49, 89	FOLKHARD	36
FITZ SIMONS	28, 56, 89	FOLSTER	67
FITZIMONS	56	FOOGE	68
FIVE	3	FOORD	3, 23, 26, 67
FIVEY	3	FOOT	3, 17, 23, 48
FLACHERTH	50	FOOTE	1, 3, 33
FLACHERTY	37	FORBIS	33, 67, 75
FLAHERTY	5, 20, 50	FORD	12, 26, 88
FLANAGAN	8, 20, 37	FORDELL	67
FLANIGAN	20, 37, 50	FORDOUN	3
FLANN	1	FOREHOUSE	87
FLANNAGAN	37, 49, 50	FOREMAN	3, 12, 23, 87
FLANNAGHAN	37, 50	FORESON	87
FLANNERY	49	FORET	75
FLANNIGAN	37, 50, 89	FORFAR	3, 21, 48, 89
FLATT	1, 71	FORGREIVE	5
FLECK	8, 37, 67	FORGUE	42
FLET	11, 15, 67	FORGY	3, 87
FLEX	75	FORK	68
FLIGHT	3, 23, 57	FORKS	68
FLIMMING	3	FORLOW	36
FLIN	8, 20, 89	FORMAN	12, 23, 26, 87
FLINN	49, 88, 89	FORRES	1, 37, 58, 85
FLINT	21, 56, 87, 88	FORRESTET	89
FLOCKART	17, 48, 67	FORSHAW	28, 33, 56, 67
FLOOD	58, 67, 71	FORSON	12, 28, 37, 87
FLORENCE	1, 47, 36	FORTAY	36
FLORIN	37	FORTEITH	53

SURNAME	DISTRICT	SURNAME	DISTRICT
FORTEVIOT	67	FRAMPTON	37, 50, 67
FORTRIETH	1	FRANK	67, 87
FORTRIETIE	1	FRANKMAN	67
FORTRIETY	1	FRANKS	87
FORTUNE	12, 26, 62, 88	FRATER	12, 36, 77, 86
FOSS	44	FRAZAR	5, 21, 71
FOSSARD	87	FRECKLETON	87
FOSSART	87	FREEBAIRN	20, 36, 37, 50
FOSSEM	(NFI) 1652, AM	FREELAND	20, 87, 88, 89
FOSSET	87	FREELANE	87
FOSSETS	87	FREELOVE	1
FOTHERGILL	67	FREEMAN	1, 5, 47, 75
FOTHERING	47, 50	FREER	87
FOTHERINGHAME	28, 56, 67	FREEVILLE	3
FOUGLER	44	FREIL	31
FOULDS	8, 20, 71	FRENCH	21, 67, 69, 88
FOULER	47, 67, 87, 88	FRESKIN	67
FOULLERTON	12	FRESKYN	67
FOULS	48, 67, 71	FRIAR	23, 28, 37, 56
FOUNTAIN	87	FRIEL	20, 37, 67
FOURNES	23	FRIEND	26, 75, 89
FOWEL	44	FRIER	26, 67, 77
FOWELL	44	FRIGG	1, 58
FOWLDS	8, 28, 56,	FRITH	1, 3, 49
FOWLER	26, 67, 75, 87	FRIZZEL	26, 28, 71
FOWLES	23, 33, 67	FROAD	8
FOWLIE	1, 11, 47	FROOD	21, 50, 88
FOWLIS	33, 48, 67	FROST	1, 47, 36
FOX	12, 36, 67, 75	FRUID	21
FOY	3, 23, 49	FUBISTER	67, 89
FOYD	3	FUDGE	34
FOYER	28, 56, 55, 89	FUKTOR	54
FOYERS	55	FULERTON	3, 5, 14
FOYT	3	FULLAR	87
FRAIER	50	FULLER	17, 67, 87, 88
FRAIL	1, 8, 83, 89	FULLON	37, 71, 89
FRAIN	1, 5	FULTEN	7
FRAINE	20	FURBER	75
FRAISER	15, 23, 26	FURBISH	DUNBAR, 1650, AM
FRAM	50, 71, 88	FURBUR	75
FRAME	37, 50, 88	FURGRIEFF	35

SURNAME	DISTRICT	SURNAME	DISTRICT
FURIE	3	GALLITY	67
FURMAGE	23, 28, 56, 75	GALLIWOOD	87
FURNESS	75	GALLOCHER	20, 37, 71
FURNIVAL	44	GALLOCK	36
FURRIE	3	GALLON	14, 35, 45, 58
FURRY	3	GALLOW	1, 47, 87
FURY	3	GALLOWATER	35
FURYE	3	GALRICK	33
FUTT	67, 71	GALRIG	33
FYVIE	1, 3, 75	GALSTON	16
FYVY	3	GALSTONE	16
GADDIE	1	GALWEY	36
GADDY	1	GALWIE	36
GADIE	11, 67, 89	GAMBLE	36, 67, 71, 89
GAFF	26, 88, 89	GAMELSON	89
GAFFNEY	23, 37, 50, 67	GAMELY	3
GAFT	45	GAMILSON	89
GAIN	37	GAMMACK	54
GAINES	37	GAMMALL	8
GAIRN	1, 11, 15	GAMMIE	1, 11, 44
GAIRNS	3, 47, 67, 69	GAMMOCK	54
GAITENS	50	GAMMY	1, 44, 49
GALACHER	23, 37, 50	GAN	15, 67, 86
GALE	1, 17, 49, 67	GANDE	86
GALEN	1, 11	GANDER	44
GALES	1	GANDIE	44
GALL	1, 3, 23	GANDY	44
GALLACHER	20, 23, 37, 50	GANE	44
GALLAGHER	8, 37, 89	GANNER	3, 23
GALLAMORE	3	GANNON	1, 23, 81, 89
GALLANT	1	GANON	23
GALLATLIE	67	GANWORTH	36
GALLATLY	67	GARDENKIRK	83
GALLETLIE	1	GARDIE	5
GALLETLY	1, 56, 67, 71	GARE	23, 28, 89
GALLIEEY	15	GAREY	1, 8, 20
GALLIERS	89	GARIE	68
GALLIEY	15	GARITY	71
GALLIMORE	3	GARL	37, 50
GALLITIE	67	GARLAND	23, 49, 88
GALLITLY	67	GARLEA	3

SURNAME	DISTRICT	SURNAME	DISTRICT
GARMACH	1	GATHERUM	33, 67
GARMAK	1, 3	GATT	75
GARMERY	21, 49, 71	GATTENS	20, 37, 50
GARMONY	21	GAUDEN	8, 89
GARNER	5	GAUDIE	1, 67, 89
GARNOCK	1, 12, 28, 56	GAUDY	1, 11, 36, 89
GARRATT	67	GAULD	1, 11, 63
GARRAWAY	36, 49, 50, 89	GAULIE	67
GARRET	8, 49, 89	GAULT	11, 50, 58
GARRETT	67	GAULTER	8
GARRIE	3, 23, 47	GAULY	67
GARRIGAN	23	GAUNT	86
GARRISON	34	GAVEN	8, 67, 71
GARRITY	28, 37, 50	GAVIN	1, 28, 47, 75
GARSCADDON	35	GAVINE	3, 23, 33, 75
GARSTANG	36	GAVINS	8, 37, 50
GARTEY	JACOBITE, 1776, AM	GAVINSON	28, 56, 89
GARTIE	85	GAVON	71
GARTLEY	36, 37, 50, 89	GAW	49, 58, 81, 89
GARTLIE	1	GAWEY	89
GARTLY	1	GAWIE	89
GARTNEY	54	GAWY	89
GARTY	85	GAY	3, 20, 23, 33, 48
GARVAN	37	GAYE	3, 23
GARVEN	8, 21, 71	GAYLOR	26, 28, 56
GARVEY	23, 47, 71	GAYNOR	37, 50
GARVIN	8, 48, 71	GAYTON	1
GARVOCH	67	GAYTONE	1
GARVOCK	67	GEALS	1
GARWOOD	83	GEBBIE	8, 50, 71
GARY	68	GEDDER	3
GAS	21, 37, 50	GEDDIE	1, 33, 58
GASCOIGNE	28, 56	GEDDIES	21, 37, 71
GASK	55, 84	GEDDIS	15, 75, 77
GASS	8, 21, 36, 49	GEEKIE	3, 23, 67
GASSOCK	36	GEEKY	3
GASTON	75	GEFFERS	33
GATENS	37, 50	GEGGIE	12, 75, 88
GATES	83	GEIKIE	28, 56
GATHERER	44	GEILS	1, 20
GATHERIM	33	GELLAM	1

SURNAME	DISTRICT	SURNAME	DISTRICT
GELLAN	1, 58	GIGHT	3
GELLATELY	3, 21, 23	GIKIE	3, 23, 33, 67
GELLATIE	67	GIKY	33
GELLATLY	3, 23, 67	GILD	89
GELLATTLY	1	GILDART	36
GELLATY	67	GILDAY	8, 37, 71
GELLEM	1	GILDEA	37, 50
GELLEN	1	GILEROY	8
GELLETLY	28, 56, 67	GILES	1, 75
GELLETTLY	1	GILESPIE	14, 37, 50
GELLILEY	33	GILFINAN	84
GELLON	1	GILGOUR	26, 71, 89
GELTSON	16	GILHAGIE	37
GEMILSTON	36	GILHAGY	37
GEMLOS	3	GILHOLM	12, 75
GEMMEL	8, 71, 88	GILIN	22
GEMMELL	8, 37, 71	GILKERSON	8, 50
GEMMIL	5, 8, 71	GILKEY	33
GENTILES	14, 50, 89	GILKIE	33
GENTLE	48, 67, 69, 81	GILLATLY	3, 23, 67
GENTLEMAN	17, 88, 89	GILLAVRY	67
GENTLES	17, 20, 87, 89	GILLDART	36
GENTRY	23, 58, 67	GILLEN	8, 50, 71
GEORGEON	15, 86, 89	GILLENDERS	1
GERAN	36	GILLES	5, 75, 89
GERAND	36	GILLIE	12, 26, 49
GERARD	1, 47, 67	GILLIESON	21
GERMAN	75	GILLIN	22
GERRAN	36, 49, 89	GILLINDERS	47
GERRAND	1, 11, 36, 89	GILLISON	21, 49, 50
GERRARD	1, 11, 67	GILLKERSON	8
GERRAT	1, 3, 49	GILLOCK	15
GERRON	8, 36, 49, 89	GILLONE	49
GERROND	49, 75, 89	GILLS	1, 11, 67
GERVIN	21, 71, 87, 89	GILLSON	3, 26, 50
GIB	3, 23, 89	GILLY	12, 26, 75
GIBBIE	8, 49, 88	GILMAN	22
GIBBINS	3, 23, 88	GILMARTIN	50
GIBBONS	3, 23, 75	GILMICHAEL	87
GIELS	1	GILMUIR	71
GIGGIE	1, 12	GILOCK	15

SURNAME	DISTRICT	SURNAME	DISTRICT
GILRAY	28, 58, 67	GLASSTER	3
GILRY	28, 56	GLASSY	23
GILSTON	28, 49, 89	GLEED	71
GILT	89	GLEG	89
GIMPSIE	36	GLEGG	1, 3, 47, 87, 89
GIMPSY	36	GLEIG	3
GIRDWOOD	28, 37, 67, 88	GLENCAIRN	67
GIRR	49	GLENCAIRNIE	85
GIRRARD	67	GLENCAIRNY	85
GIRRIE	1, 11	GLENCORE	36
GIRTWOOD	83	GLENCORSE	21, 49
GIRVAN	8, 16, 49, 89	GLENCROSS	21, 49, 50
GIRVANE	16	GLENDAY	3, 23
GIRWOOD	83	GLENDEY	3
GIVAN	12, 75, 89	GLENDIE	3, 23
GIVANS	75	GLENDY	3, 67
GIVEN	33, 67, 71, 87	GLENESK	3
GIVENS	87	GLENHOLM	83
GLADSTON	12, 75, 77	GLENHOLME	83
GLADSTONE	21, 67, 75	GLENISON	1
GLADSTONES	21, 28, 75	GLESSEN	67
GLAISHER	3	GLINDINNING	JACOBITE, 1716, AM
GLAISTER	3	GLOAG	23, 28, 67, 84
GLAMES	3	GLOAK	84
GLANCE	87	GLOAKS	84
GLANCEY	37, 50	GLOVER	3, 7, 21, 49
GLANCY	37, 71, 89	GOALEN	28, 47, 56
GLANDIE	67	GODALL	26, 75
GLANDY	67	GODDARD	1, 28, 75, 89
GLASBORO	23	GODFREYSON	83
GLASBOROW	23	GODMAN	34
GLASER	3	GODRICKSON	87
GLASFORD	83	GODSMAN	1, 3, 34, 44,
GLASGO	37	GODWIN	8, 28, 56
GLASGOW	26, 28, 37, 88	GOFERS	33
GLASHEN	1, 33, 58	GOGAR	87
GLASSEL	28, 56	GOGGIN	87
GLASSELL	67	GOGGINS	87
GLASSFORD	37, 50, 71, 80	GOLD	3, 17, 50
GLASSIE	23	GOLDER	3
GLASSITER	3	GOLDIE	8, 21, 36, 49

SURNAME	DISTRICT	SURNAME	DISTRICT
GOLDING	28, 56, 88	GORRY	15, 23, 67
GOLDMAN	23	GORTHIE	67
GOLDSMAN	1	GORTIE	67
GOLDSMITH	83	GORTY	67
GOLDY	36	GOSFORD	62
GOLIGHTLY	8, 12, 26, 67	GOSKIRK	28, 56, 67, 87
GOLLACH	86	GOSMAN	28, 33, 89
GOLLAND	33	GOSPATRICK	22
GOLLIE	1, 8	GOSSIP	1, 58
GOLSPIE	86	GOTTERSON	3, 12, 75
GOMM	87	GOUCK	3
GOOD	8, 12, 37, 49	GOUDIE	8, 67, 89
GOODAL	11, 26, 67	GOUGH	23, 28, 56
GOODALE	11, 26, 33	GOUGHAN	37, 50
GOODALL	28, 33, 75	GOUINLOCK	21
GOODBODY	44	GOUK	3, 23, 47
GOODBRAND	1, 11	GOULD	3, 26, 33, 67
GOODE	37	GOULDIE	8, 58, 89
GOODFELLOW	3, 47, 75, 77	GOURDAN	DUNBAR, 1650, AM
GOODLAD	81, 89	GOURDIE	33, 67
GOODLATTE	89	GOURLIE	12, 50, 83, 89
GOODMAN	47, 49, 89	GOURLY	83
GOODSMAN	1, 28, 56	GOURTON	87
GOODWILL	3, 12, 67	GOUSSE	28
GOODWILLIE	23, 33, 67	GOVAN	20, 37, 50
GOODWILLY	33	GOVANS	37
GOODWIN	20, 81, 83, 89	GOVE	1, 3, 47
GOOLD	3, 37, 50, 88	GOVENLOCK	75, 77
GOOLSPIE	86	GOWANLOCK	21, 28, 75, 87
GOPELL	12, 28, 56	GOWDIE	37, 50, 89
GORDEN	1, 47, 89	GOWENLOCK	21, 75, 77
GORHAM	17, 28, 67	GOWER	37, 50, 89
GORIE	23, 33, 67	GOWIE	11, 33, 63
GORLET	35	GOWK	3
GORLETT	35	GOWLOCK	1, 89
GORLY	33, 83	GOWRIE	1, 3, 20
GORMACK	1, 67	GRACE	23, 49, 56, 67
GORMAND	8, 26, 89	GRADEN	75, 87
GORME	67	GRADENE	87
GORO	37	GRADY	28, 50, 56
GORRIE	17, 67, 69	GRAHAMSLAW	31

SURNAME	DISTRICT	SURNAME	DISTRICT
GRAHME	14, 23, 37	GRICE	28, 37, 56
GRAINGER	28, 75, 88, 89	GRIEG	14, 23, 33
GRAINS	44	GRIEVER	75
GRANDISON	26, 33, 88	GRIEVES	3, 12, 75
GRANDISTOUN	3	GRIFFEN	3, 8, 37, 89
GRANDY	1, 3, 23	GRIFFIN	37, 50, 89
GRANGER	48, 50, 67, 75	GRIFFITHS	28, 56, 71
GRANTHAM	17, 36	GRIGORY	1
GRANTHAME	36	GRIMSON	50, 67
GRATNEY	54	GRINDISON	26, 33
GRAUNT	DUNBAR, 1650, AM	GRINDLAY	20, 87, 88, 89
GRAVES	21, 37, 88	GRINDLEY	37, 71, 87, 88
GREADY	37, 50, 89	GRINDLIE	87
GREAM	3, 20, 49	GRINDLY	87
GREARSON	5, 12, 21	GRINDY	26
GREAS	68	GRINLAW	12
GREAT	15, 23, 67	GRINLEY	17, 33, 56
GREATHEAD	1, 11, 15, 75, 89	GRINOCK	8
GREENAWAY	37, 50, 89	GRINTON	28, 33, 56, 87
GREENE	12, 28, 58, 75	GRISSELL	COVENANTER, 1685, AM
GREENHEAD	87	GRIVE	20, 33, 77
GREENHILL	3, 67, 88	GROSART	67, 83, 88, 89
GREENHILLS	3	GROSERT	12, 56, 75
GREENHORN	50, 88, 89	GROSSART	28, 56, 67
GREENLESS	5, 37, 71	GROSSAT	1, 12, 71
GREENOCK	8, 28, 56, 88	GROUNDWATER	1, 44, 48, 67
GREENSHIELDS	37, 50, 88, 89	GROVE	17, 28, 37
GREENWOOD	1, 44, 75, 88	GROVES	37, 71, 87, 89
GREEVE	33, 67, 77	GROWAR	3, 23
GREGGAN	49	GROZART	33, 56, 89
GREIGG	1, 89	GRUB	23, 33, 47
GREIR	8, 37, 71	GRUBB	3, 23, 33
GREIVE	26, 48, 55, 75	GRUBBE	3
GRENDLEY	87	GRUBBET	75
GRENDLIE	87	GRUNTON	8
GRENDON	1	GUALD	3, 23, 67
GRESOUN	1	GUALTER	DUNBAR, 1650, AM
GREVAR	67	GUELP	1
GREVER	67	GUELPH	1
GRIACH	1	GUIDING	87
GRIBBIN	21, 37, 50		

SURNAME	DISTRICT	SURNAME	DISTRICT
GUILLAN	3, 23, 33	HADDO	36
GUILMETTE	36	HADDOCK	8, 71, 78, 89
GULLAN	12, 33, 56, 62	HADDOW	8, 50, 83, 88
GULLAND	28, 33, 48, 62	HADDOWAY	37, 83
GULLANE	62	HADYARD	83
GULLEN	21, 26, 89	HAEDRIDGE	28
GULLIAN	3, 23	HAFFIE	37, 49, 89
GULLIOIN	67	HAGA	23
GULLON	26, 88, 89	HAGAN	37
GUNIM	36	HAGARTY	20, 37, 71
GUNNING	21, 23, 37, 49	HAGE	DUNBAR, 1650, AM
GUNNION	8, 49, 89	HAGELIE	56
GUNNYON	1, 21, 49	HAGEN	37
GUNYON	8	HAGERTY	37, 50, 71
GUNZEON	49	HAGGAN	33, 37, 50
GURLY	89	HAGGARD	5, 45, 67
GURNAY	75	HAGGARTY	37, 50, 71
GURNER	75	HAGGAS	23
GURNEY	75	HAGGERT	3, 23, 67
GURRAN	36	HAGGERTY	12, 37, 50
GURRAND	36	HAGGIE	17, 48, 67, 89
GUTHEL	3, 47, 48	HAGGINS	50, 67, 89
GUTHERIE	20, 33, 89	HAGGIS	23
GUTHRY	8, 33, 49	HAGGON	50
GUTRIDG	DUNBAR, 1650, AM	HAGOMAN	87
GUY	20, 26, 71	HAGSTON	87
GUYAN	1, 47	HAGSTOUN	87
GUYLER	37, 50	HAIGS	21, 33
HABBICK	33	HAILEY	28, 37, 71
HACHIE	3	HAILSTONES	50, 56, 88
HACHY	3	HAIN	11, 33, 49
HACKET	33	HAINAN	8
HACKIE	3	HAINE	28, 45, 56
HACKING	36	HAINES	8, 37, 49
HACKLAND	67	HAINEY	21, 49, 89
HACKSTONE	COVENANTER, 1678, AM	HAINING	8, 21, 49, 67
HACKY	3	HAINNING	21, 49, 89
HADDEM	36	HAINSON	5, 33
HADDIE	21, 50, 88	HAIRSTAINES	36
HADDINGTON	37	HAIRSTAINS	21, 36
HADDLE	85	HAIRSTENS	21

SURNAME	DISTRICT	SURNAME	DISTRICT
HAIRSTONES	50	HAMPSEY	8
HAISTINGS	8	HAMPSIE	8
HAITLEY	33	HAMPSON	3, 23, 47
HAITLIE	36	HAMPTON	3, 23, 37, 47
HAITLY	36	HANAH	37, 50, 71
HALBERT	8, 21, 50, 68	HANAMAN	3
HALCROSS	44	HAND	23, 37, 50
HALFKNIGHT	87	HANDIE	23
HALFORD	44	HANDLIE	36
HALFPENNY	8, 37, 87, 88	HANDLING	21, 23, 47
HALHEAD	23	HANDLY	20, 36, 37, 49
HALIDAY	12, 21, 49	HANDMAN	5
HALKERSON	87	HANDS	28, 37, 56
HALKETS	89	HANDY	23
HALLAM	44	HANDYSIDE	28, 56, 77, 87
HALLEM	44	HANKIN	1
HALLEY	48, 55, 63, 67	HANKINSON	28, 56
HALLIDAY	12, 21, 36, 49, 50	HANLEY	44, 49, 81, 89
HALLIE	67, 55	HANLIE	44
HALLISON	87	HANLIN	37, 49, 88
HALLIWELL	75	HANLON	28, 37, 50
HALLON	71	HANLY	20, 21, 56
HALLOWAY	8, 50, 71	HANNAM	75
HALLOWELL	71, 75, 77	HANNAN	14, 26, 56
HALLSON	87	HANNAWINKLE	87
HALLY	17, 55, 67, 75	HANNING	21, 49, 75, 89
HALLYBURTON	33, 67, 86	HANOMAN	3
HALSON	3, 23, 33, 87	HANRATTIE	36, 87
HALSTON	28, 50, 56	HANRATTY	36, 87
HALTON	36	HANSEN	9, 37, 50
HALVIE	36	HANSON	28, 81, 85, 89
HALVY	36	HANTON	3, 23, 47
HAMBLY	75	HAPPER	12, 89
HAMEL	26, 71, 89	HAPPLE	8, 37, 50
HAMER	83	HAPPY	83
HAMIL	37, 49, 50	HARBATTLE	56
HAMMAR	37	HARBOTTLE	28
HAMMER	37	HARCASE	87
HAMMIL	37, 50	HARCOS	87
HAMMOND	3, 23, 37, 49	HARCUS	49, 67, 87, 88
HAMMONDS	23	HARDCASTLE	75

SURNAME	DISTRICT	SURNAME	DISTRICT
HARDEN	8, 23, 50, 75	HARTLEY	20, 28, 36, 89
HARDING	67	HARTLIE	36
HARDLEY	53	HARTNESS	8
HARDLIE	53	HARTON	8, 47, 56
HARDLY	53	HARTSIDE	83
HARDWICK	37	HARTY	8, 12
HARENS	28, 56, 67	HARWOOD	35
HARESON	26, 89	HASBEN	3
HARG	36	HASLAN	28, 56
HARGEAVES	36	HASSAN	37
HARGRAVE	3, 7	HASSELL	87
HARKEN	50, 71, 75	HASSELT	44
HARKENSS	67	HASSEN	37
HARKER	3, 8, 23	HASSENDEAN	75
HARKES	15, 26, 67, 69	HASTAN	36
HARKESS	87	HASTANE	36
HARKIN	20, 71, 77	HASTON	33, 56, 88
HARKINS	8, 37, 50	HASWELL	12, 20, 75, 89
HARLAND	23, 26, 33	HATCHET	33
HARLAW	42	HATCHETTE	33
HARLEY	42, 17, 33, 48	HATELIE	12, 88
HARLIE	42	HATELY	12, 26, 75
HARLOW	42	HATHAWAY	32
HARMAN	21, 33, 89	HATHCOCK	36
HARMER	83	HATHERN	81, 89
HARNESS	83	HATHINGTON	87
HARON	21, 71, 89	HATHORN	8, 49, 89
HAROWER	33, 67	HATLEY	12, 28, 75
HARPERFIELD	83	HATLIE	67, 77
HARRA	8, 49, 71	HATLLIE	50
HARRAH	71	HATSTON	15
HARRAY	67, 89	HATT	1, 47
HARRIER	5, 26, 33	HATTO	75
HARRIGAN	8, 20, 89	HATTON	23, 33, 49
HARRON	33, 45, 89	HATTRICK	37, 50, 71
HARROT	87	HAUGHIE	37
HARROWAY	87	HAUGHY	37
HART	71, 75, 77	HAWICK	40, 71, 75 89
HARTE	75	HAWK	33
HARTFELL	67	HAWKINS	21, 44, 75, 89
HARTIN	1	HAWKSELY	1

SURNAME	DISTRICT	SURNAME	DISTRICT
HAWLEY	87	HEDDERWICK	22, 28, 37, 48
HAXON	87	HEDDIE	33, 50, 67
HAYCOCK	28, 56	HEDDLE	28, 67, 86
HAYHURST	86	HEDDLESTON	21, 28, 49
HAYMAN	5, 8, 14	HEDDLIE	44
HAYROCK	85	HEDERICK	22
HAZEL	3, 8, 23	HEDLEY	26, 75, 89
HAZELL	44	HEGERTY	8, 20, 37, 50
HAZELS	3	HEGGARTY	8, 37, 50
HAZELS	23	HEGGERTY	33, 37, 50
HAZELWOOD	3, 23, 28	HEIDSHOIP	79
HAZLITT	25	HEIGH	3, 28, 33
HEADER	22	HEITH	3, 23, 75
HEADRICK	17, 33, 67	HEITON	37, 50, 75
HEADRIDGE	67, 89	HELEM	75
HEALL	71	HELEN	15, 49, 89
HEALY	3, 23, 50	HELLIWELL	28, 56
HEAN	3, 23, 47	HELLON	20, 21, 89
HEARD	21, 58, 77	HELM	67, 75, 77
HEARIE	23	HELMRICH	1
HEARLD	3	HELMS	75
HEART	75	HEMINGWAY	1
HEARY	23	HEMISTON	34
HEASLETT	14	HEMMING	36
HEASTIE	21, 89	HEMMINGS	36
HEASTIN	28	HEMMISTON	34
HEATH	17, 28, 44, 77	HEMPSEED	33, 88, 89
HEATHERSGILL	79	HEMPSON	28, 56, 89
HEATHFIELD	75	HENCHAN	36
HEATLEY	33, 75, 88	HENCHEN	36
HEATLIE	12, 36, 75, 77, 87	HENEY	37, 49, 50
HEATLY	12, 26, 36, 56, 87	HENNEY	20, 49, 89
HEBBENTON	3	HENSCHEL	83
HEBRON	3, 8, 23, 87	HENSHAW	37, 50, 71, 75
HECKFORD	75	HENSHELWOOD	37, 50, 83, 75
HECTOR	1, 47	HENWOOD	5, 77
HECTORSON	85	HENY	28, 49, 77
HEDDEL	67	HERBERT	89
HEDDELL	44	HERBERTSON	21, 37, 62, 77
HEDDER	22	HERCULESON	89
HEDDERICK	WORCESTER, 1651, AM	HERCUS	15, 67

SURNAME	DISTRICT	SURNAME	DISTRICT
HERD	3, 33, 36, 63	HEWIT	12, 28, 49
HERDMAN	3, 28, 56, 67	HEWITSON	21, 67, 75
HERING	22, 37, 50	HEWITT	1, 12, 49, 35
HERKES	26, 56, 67, 87	HEYWOOD	85
HERKESS	26, 56	HIBBERT	44
HERKIS	26, 37, 56, 67	HICKEY	20, 37, 71
HERMISTON	12, 75	HICKMAN	56, 67
HERN	89	HICKS	1, 14, 86, 89
HERRIN	26, 50, 89	HIDDLES	33
HERRING	8, 23, 22, 75, 88	HIDDLESTON	21, 36, 49, 89
HERRINGTON	33, 35	HIGBEN	WORCESTER, 1651, AM
HERRIS	21, 47, 67	HIGGEN	17, 33, 89
HERRSHILL	3	HIGGENS	23, 81, 89
HERSCHEL	3	HIGGIE	23, 33, 89
HERSCHELL	3	HIGGIN	8, 37, 50
HERSH	87	HIGGINS	17, 37, 89
HERSHELL	3	HIGH	3, 23, 33
HERSHILL	3	HIGHEN	87
HERSHTON	87	HIGHET	8, 37, 49, 71
HERSTON	87	HIGHGATE	37
HERUS	26	HIGHLAND	20, 81, 89
HERVO	34	HIGHLANDS	37, 50, 89
HERVOE	34	HIGNAT	67
HERWART	87	HIGNATT	67
HESSON	37, 67, 89	HIGNET	67
HESTER	37, 50	HIGNETT	67
HETHERINGTON	21, 49, 75, 88	HIGNIGHT	67
HETHERTON	21, 28, 88	HIGNIT	67
HETHERWICK	87	HIGNITE	67
HETHRINGTON	37, 49, 50	HIGNITT	67
HEUCHEN	36	HIGNUT	67
HEUGH	33, 88, 89	HILCOAT	37, 50, 71
HEUGHAN	21, 49, 89	HILHOUSE	8, 37, 71
HEVER	44	HILL	3, 21, 75, 88
HEWAT	1, 12, 28, 35, 75	HILLAN	37, 50
HEWATSON	21, 49, 50	HILLARY	44
HEWATT	26, 50, 89	HILLERY	44
HEWDEN	44	HILLHOUSE	8, 20, 37, 50
HEWETSON	21, 36, 49, 89	HILLOCK	37
HEWETT	1, 35	HILLOCKS	3, 23
HEWIE	12, 26	HILLS	12, 75, 77

SURNAME	DISTRICT	SURNAME	DISTRICT
HILLSON	12, 20, 26	HODGET	37
HILSON	12, 67, 75, 83	HODGETON	3
HILSTON	28, 50	HODGSON	5, 21, 49
HILTON	11, 37, 67, 87	HODGSTON	3, 37, 50
HINCHLIFF	1, 21	HOG	17, 75, 77, 87
HIND	17, 33, 37, 88	HOGAN	33, 48, 49
HINDE	37	HOGART	1, 71
HINDLE	21, 71	HOGG	68
HINDMAN	68	HOGGAN	33, 48, 87, 89
HINDMARSH	23, 58, 75	HOGGANS	20, 28, 56
HINE	75	HOGGARTH	12, 14, 75
HINES	75	HOLBROOK	28, 56
HINSHAW	75	HOLBURN	8, 28, 89
HINSHELWOOD	37, 71, 75, 80	HOLCOTT	75
HIPSON	56	HOLDEN	3, 12, 21, 33
HIRD	1, 11, 47	HOLDFORTH	67
HIRDMAN	3	HOLDIN	3
HIRR	36	HOLE	36
HIRSEL	87	HOLGATE	1, 37
HIRSELL	87	HOLLAND	3, 8, 26, 67
HIRST	87	HOLLIDAY	12, 21, 36, 49
HIRSTON	87	HOLLINGER	44
HISLOP	67, 75, 77	HOLLIS	21, 28, 71
HISTON	12	HOLLIWELL	75
HITCHELL	3, 47, 36, 49	HOLLOWAY	75
HITSON	8	HOLM	DUNBAR, 1650, AM
HITT	33	HOLME	1, 45
HNICHLIFF	1	HOLMS	49, 71, 89
HOARE	8, 28, 56, 88	HOLYWELL	12, 26, 28
HOASACK	75	HOMER	36
HOATSON	21, 49, 71	HONEY	3, 23, 67
HOBART	3, 8, 23, 75	HOOD	5, 8, 12, 26, 87
HOBB	1, 3, 47	HOOK	12, 28, 36, 56
HOBBS	1, 49, 89	HOOKE	36
HOCUTT	75	HOOPER	12, 33, 75
HODDAM	36	HOPKIN	8, 20, 23, 89
HODGE	33, 37, 67, 89	HOPKINS	8, 20, 23, 47
HODGEON	50	HOPPER	12, 21, 75, 87
HODGERT	50, 71	HOPPRINGLE	35
HODGES	37, 89	HOPSON	8, 26, 37, 56
HODGESON	8	HORAN	5

SURNAME	DISTRICT	SURNAME	DISTRICT
HORDEN	83	HOWARTH	1, 20, 47
HOREN	5	HOWAT	8, 21, 49
HORLEY	1	HOWATSON	8, 21, 49, 87
HORLIE	1	HOWATT	21, 33, 71
HORLY	1	HOWBURN	36
HORMEL	36	HOWES	3, 23, 28
HORMELL	36	HOWEY	3, 23, 75
HORN	11, 20, 48	HOWIESON	17, 33, 50
HORNAL	21, 49, 50	HOWILSTON	88
HORNE	12, 15, 67	HOWITSON	21, 37, 50
HORNEL	21, 28, 49	HOWITT	11, 20, 71
HORNELL	36	HOWKINS	28, 56
HORNER	3	HOWLISTON	12, 56
HORNSBY	45, 49, 89	HOWNAM	RIOTER, 1750, AM
HORRAN	5	HOWNAME	79
HORREN	5	HOWNAN	75
HORTON	11, 23, 37	HOWNANE	75
HOSE	8, 37, 50, 87	HOWSON	87
HOSEA	1, 3, 47	HOWSTON	8, 17, 21
HOSEASON	3, 89	HOWTON	83
HOSEY	1, 3, 23, 50	HOY	15, 33, 48, 75, 77
HOSICK	3, 12, 23	HOYE	15, 75
HOSIE	1, 23, 37, 89	HOYLE	67
HOSIER	5, 28, 67	HOZACK	58, 63, 67
HOSSACK	11, 58	HOZIER	28, 50, 56
HOSSIE	3, 20, 23	HUBBARD	44
HOSTLER	3, 28, 33	HUBBERD	44
HOTCHKIS	21, 67, 89	HUCHAN	36
HOTSON	21, 50, 75	HUCHEON	1, 33
HOUD	3, 75	HUCHIN	36
HOUDEN	12, 26, 89	HUCHISON	15, 37, 67
HOUGHTON	83	HUDDLESTON	1, 49, 67
HOULISON	20, 26, 37	HUDDLESTONE	67
HOULISTON	12, 37, 67, 75	HUGH	33, 47, 88
HOUN	1	HUGHAN	21, 36, 49, 89
HOUNAM	75	HUGHES	44, 49, 67, 89
HOUSTAN	15, 20, 71	HUGHS	33, 37, 71
HOUSTEN	15, 20, 89	HUGS	33
HOVELL	23	HULDIE	68
HOW	3, 12, 23	HULDY	68
HOWARD	14, 20, 63	HULK	1

SURNAME	DISTRICT	SURNAME	DISTRICT
HULT	3	HYNDEFORD	83
HULTON	87	HYNDMAN	68
HUMBLE	12, 47, 75	HYNDS	37, 50
HUMIL	33	HYNE	89
HUMILL	33	HYNE	28, 88
HUMMIL	33	HYSLOP	21, 49, 89
HUMMILL	33	IBBOTSON	74
HUMPHARSON	37	IDILL	1
HUMPHARSTON	37	IDVIE	3
HUMPHRAY	8, 58, 89	IDVY	3
HUMPHREY	1, 8, 47	ILAK	1
HUMPHRIES	28, 56	ILIFE	33
HUMPHRY	8, 11, 47	ILIFFE	33
HUNLIE	42	ILLINGWORTH	44
HUNNAM	87	ILROE	8
HUNTINGDON	36	ILROWE	8
HUNTLIE	42	IMBART	75
HUNTON	3, 67, 89	IMBERT	75
HURD	58, 86, 89	IMBRIE	8, 37, 50
HURL	37, 50	IMBRY	8
HUSBAND	3, 23, 33, 69, 87	IMLACH	1
HUSE	87	IMLAH	1, 11, 67
HUSH	12, 15, 75, 87	IMLAY	1, 67, 89
HUT	67	IMRAY	1, 47
HUTCHEN	3, 11, 67	IMREY	12, 37, 47, 67
HUTCHEON	1, 47, 58	IMRIE	23, 33, 67, 84
HUTCHESON	17, 67, 71	INAN	21
HUTCHIE	23, 47, 88	INCHMARTIN	67
HUTCHIESON	71, 88, 89	ING	36
HUTCHINGS	28, 56	INGHAM	14, 28, 89
HUTCHINS	28, 37, 56	INGLAND	1, 11, 67
HUTCHON	3, 58	INGLESTON	67
HUTCON	33	INGREM	1, 58, 89
HUTSON	14, 67, 77	INKSETER	89
HUTT	33, 67	INKSETTER	67, 75
HUXLEY	44	INMAN	1
HUXLY	44	INNERDALE	3
HYLAND	41	INNERWICK	22
HYMERS	75, 77, 86	INSCH	11, 58
HYND	17, 23, 33	INSH	58
HYNDE	37	INSHAW	37

SURNAME	DISTRICT	SURNAME	DISTRICT
INSTANT	26, 28, 56	JEFFERIES	28, 56, 75
INVERARITY	3, 23, 71, 87	JEFFERIS	75
INVERDALE	3	JEFFERS	75
IRELAND	33, 44, 49, 67, 84	JEFFERSON	35
IRON	3, 71, 75	JEFFRAY	50, 77, 89
IRONS	3, 23, 67	JEFFREYS	12, 28, 56
IRONSIDE	1, 11	JEFFRIES	1
ISABELL	28	JEFFS	28, 50, 56
ISABELLA	1, 75	JELLIE	36
ISBESTER	28, 67, 89	JELLY	3, 36, 88, 89
ISBUSTER	89	JEMPSON	DUNBAR, 1650, AM
ISDALE	17, 48, 67, 75	JENKIN	3, 11, 60, 89
ISDALL	75	JENKINS	3, 20, 37, 58
IVAR	ARGYLL'S REBELLION, 1685, AM	JENKINSON	26, 28, 56
		JENNER	20, 28, 56, 87
IZATT	17, 33, 50	JENNETT	44
IZETT	28, 33, 56	JENNETTE	44
JACK	1, 15, 23, 75	JENNINGS	28, 37, 50
JACKS	1	JENSON	3
JACKSON	21, 37, 44, 48, 67	JERDON	37, 50, 75
JACOB	3	JERRAT	67
JACOBS	3	JERRATE	67
JACOBSON	3, 45, 71, 89	JERRET	33, 71, 89
JAFFERY	75	JERRETT	67
JAFFRAY	1, 63, 89	JERRETTE	67
JAFFREY	12, 75, 89	JERVEY	87
JAMES	11, 44, 58, 63	JERVIE	28, 48, 87, 89
JAMIE	3, 8, 47, 83	JERVIS	3, 26, 33, 86, 87
JAMNELL	WORCESTER, 1652, AM	JERVY	82
JAPP	3, 33, 47	JESS	1, 21, 36, 89
JAROMSON	89	JESSAMIN	11
JARRON	3, 23	JESSAMINE	1, 11
JARVEY	20, 37, 89	JESSOP	3, 21
JARVIE	20, 67, 89	JIMSON	WORCESTER, 1652, AM
JARVIS	3, 33, 47, 89	JINKIN	81, 89
JASPER	1	JINKINS	23, 58, 89
JASS	3, 11, 58	JIRKCALDY	12
JAYNER	75	JOASS	1, 9, 11
JEANS	1, 58	JOBSON	3, 23, 67, 75
JEBB	36	JOCK	28, 56, 67
JEFF	68	JOE	3

SURNAME	DISTRICT	SURNAME	DISTRICT
JOHN	45, 48, 49	KEANE	17, 37, 89
JOHNMAN	48, 67	KEARLIE	44
JOHNS	14, 36, 45, 67	KEARLY	44
JOINER	1, 11, 88	KEARNEY	20, 21, 71, 89
JOLLIE	3, 17, 20, 47	KEARNIE	37, 50, 75
JOLLY	1, 3, 47, 36	KEATING	20, 28, 37
JONES	8, 26, 37	KEDIE	28, 56, 75
JOOHNMAN	33	KEDSLIE	23, 26, 28
JOPSON	67	KEDZLIE	28, 56
JORDAN	1, 12, 75, 89	KEELLY	82
JORIE	36	KEELY	82
JOURDAN	1	KEEN	21, 33, 47
JOURDEN	1	KEENAN	28, 36, 37, 56
JOY	44	KEER	14, 33, 89
JOYCE	8, 28, 44, 89	KEGO	71
JOYNER	1, 75	KEIFF	33
JOYS	44	KEIGAN	23, 37, 50
JUDHOPE	29, 37	KEILAR	37, 67, 89
JUDSON	87	KEILER	3, 23, 33
JUNER	20, 45, 58	KEILL	3, 26, 47
JUNES	1	KEILLAR	3, 23, 67
JUNIOR	44	KEILLER	54, 23, 33, 67
JUNKEIN	28, 71	KEILLOR	3, 23, 67
JUNKEN	8, 67, 75	KEILOH	1
JUNKIN	3, 58, 89	KEILOR	3, 23, 54, 67
JUNKINS	58	KEIN	28
JUNKISON	26, 28, 56	KEIR	11, 33, 89
JUNNER	53, 45, 58, 63	KEIRD	85
JUNOR	44, 45, 63, 75	KEISER	28, 56
JUST	3, 23, 33	KELBURN	74
JUSTICE	23, 33, 67	KELHAM	5
KAINE	50, 71	KELL	37, 49, 50, 87
KAIR	21, 47, 89	KELLET	21, 28, 56
KANDOW	3	KELLMAN	1
KARRICK	16	KELLOCK	17, 21, 33
KAYES	8	KELLS	36
KAYLER	54	KELMAN	1, 11
KAYLOR	54	KELMARTIN	33
KEA	3, 15, 21	KELMIN	1
KEADDY	36	KELSALL	87
KEAND	5, 36, 49, 89	KELSAY	75

SURNAME	DISTRICT	SURNAME	DISTRICT
KELSELL	87	KENNOCK	33
KELSO	7, 8, 14, 71, 75	KENNON	14, 49, 88
KELT	23, 37, 67, 89	KENNOUGH	JACOBITE, 1747, AM
KELTIE	8, 17, 38, 48, 89	KENNY	3, 23, 37
KELTON	21, 36, 49, 89	KENT	50, 56, 62, 67, 89
KELTY	33, 48, 67, 87	KEOGH	37, 50
KELVIE	5, 49, 89	KEOT	89
KELVIN	37	KEPPEL	26
KEMBO	89	KEPPEN	67, 89
KEMLO	1, 3, 47	KEPPY	26, 28, 56
KEMLOUGH	3	KERCHOPE	3, 75
KEMLY	3	KERMATH	3, 23, 67
KEMP	1, 11, 67	KERRAY	68
KEMPER	WORCESTER, 1652, AM	KERRIE	68
KEMPIE	67, 89	KERRIGAN	50, 71, 89
KEMPLIN	53	KERROW	20, 67
KEMPSTER	67	KERSE	12, 75, 89
KEMPT	1, 45	KERSS	12, 75
KEMPY	67, 89	KERWIN	32
KEN	36	KESBIE	44
KENAN	36	KESBY	44
KENAPER	62	KESSACK	11
KENGHAN	36	KESSEN	47, 50, 71, 80
KENLOCH	33	KESSIE	50, 89
KENLOCK	33	KESSON	1, 17, 47, 83
KENMORE	67	KETCHAN	28, 56
KENMOUGH	33	KETHEL	67
KENMUIR	8, 67, 89	KETTELS	67
KENMURE	8, 49, 67, 89	KETTLE	48, 56, 67, 84
KENN	36	KETTLES	17, 23, 67, 84
KENNA	8, 49, 89,	KETTLESON	89
KENNAN	49, 88, 89	KETTLESTON	89
KENNEDAY	49, 50, 71	KEUNAN	36
KENNEL	36	KEVAN	36, 37, 49, 89
KENNESON	3, 23, 33	KEVEN	36
KENNET	20	KEVIN	36
KENNIDAY	49	KIBBLE	68
KENNIDY	1, 67, 88	KID	26, 48, 88
KENNIE	(NFI) 1685, AM	KIDDY	12, 33, 67
KENNING	34	KIDSTOUN	19
KENNOCH	67	KIEL	71

SURNAME	DISTRICT	SURNAME	DISTRICT
KIELAN	44	KINGREE	87
KIELLER	3, 23	KINGRY	87
KIER	17, 67, 89	KINGSTON	5, 37, 50
KIETH	5, 20, 67	KINIMONTH	67
KILBRIDE	37, 50, 71	KINMENT	67
KILBURN	74	KINMINT	88
KILCULLAN	3	KINMOND	3, 23, 67
KILCULLEN	3	KINNA	36
KILDONAN	8	KINNABURGH	37
KILES	16	KINNAH	67
KILL	21, 71, 89	KINNAMONT	37, 50
KILLAN	5, 8, 67	KINNEBURG	37
KILLDAY	37, 50	KINNEL	33, 49, 89
KILLEN	8, 17, 89	KINNESON	67, 71
KILLIGAN	21, 28, 56	KINNETH	33, 47
KILLIN	37, 56, 89	KINNEY	50, 71, 89
KILLOCH	11, 71, 89	KINNIBURGH	20, 37, 50, 86
KILLOCK	11, 21, 71	KINNIMOND	23
KILMAN	1, 3, 47	KINNIMONT	28, 56, 71
KILNER	87	KINNINMOND	67
KILOH	1, 11	KINNISON	3, 23, 67
KILREA	8	KINSMAN	5, 33, 37
KILREE	8	KINSMAND	87
KILTIE	36	KINSTRAY	21, 49
KIMMERHAME	87	KINSTRY	21, 49, 71
KIMMERHOME	87	KIPHART	36
KIMMIT	3, 23	KIPP	83
KINAH	67	KIPPEN	56, 67, 77, 89
KINARD	89	KIPPIE	28, 36, 37, 50
KINART	89	KIRBY	87
KINBUCK	87	KIRDIE	74
KINCAIRD	8	KIRDY	74
KINCRAIGIE	1	KIRKBRIDE	36
KINCRAIGY	1	KIRKBRIGHT	36
KINDAL	36	KIRKBY	87
KINDALL	36	KIRKBYE	87
KINDLER	23	KIRKCONNEL	21, 49
KINGAN	37, 49, 89	KIRKCUP	3
KINGARTH	84	KIRKE	17, 21, 49
KINGEN	49	KIRKHAM	21, 33, 37
KINGERY	87	KIRKHOP	8, 50

SURNAME	DISTRICT	SURNAME	DISTRICT
KIRKHOPE	3, 21, 56, 67	LACKIE	21, 47, 89
KIRKPATRIC	50	LACKLAND	75
KIRKTON	1, 11, 75	LACKY	28
KIRKTOUN	75	LACY	1, 71
KIRKUP	3	LADDEN	1
KIRKWALL	(NFI) 1685, AM	LADEN	1
KIRSOP	53, 87	LADLEY	DUNBAR, 1650, AM
KIRTON	1, 47	LADLEY	8, 49, 89
KIRWEN	32	LADYARD	87
KISSACH	JACOBITE, 1747, AM	LADYURD	87
KITCHEN	1, 58, 67	LAFFERTY	37, 50, 88
KITSON	89	LAFFRIES	44
KITTELS	3, 23	LAFFRYS	44
KITTLES	3, 17, 67	LAG	36
KIVEN	37	LAGE	36
KLED	36	LAGGS	36
KNARSTON	3, 23, 67	LAGHEAD	83
KNIGHT	3, 47, 67	LAGS	36
KNOTTERBELT	44	LAHOAR	37
KNOWES	26	LAHORE	37
KNOWLEN	44	LAIDLEY	21, 56, 89
KNOWLES	1, 54, 47, 88	LAIKIE	3
KNOWLIN	44	LAILER	80
KOON	8	LAKE	28, 50, 67
KRAIL	33	LALLIE	75
KRAMER	44	LALLY	75
KRETH	36	LAMBDEN	87
KROLL	23	LAMBE	8, 71, 89
KRON	5	LAMBER	17, 48, 77
KUGAN	36	LAMBERTON	8, 12, 37, 87
KULP	1	LAMBETH	3, 23
KURD	85	LAMINGTON	83
KUTCHEON	48, 63, 77	LAMLIE	22
KYAN	28, 56	LAMLY	22
KYD	3, 23, 33	LAMMONT	21, 67, 89
KYLIE	28, 50, 89	LAMP	36
KYNAH	JACOBITE, 1747, AM	LAMPE	36
KYND	3, 15, 23	LAMPO	LIBEL, 1751, AM
KYNDNESS	1	LANARK	83
LABURN	3	LANCASTER	21, 26, 89
LACHORE	8	LANCEMAN	3

SURNAME	DISTRICT	SURNAME	DISTRICT
LAND	8, 26, 71	LATTIMORE	36
LANDALS	26, 56, 67	LATTO	1, 26, 33, 68
LANDELLS	12, 21, 33	LAUBHLAN	50
LANDES	8, 37	LAUCHLIN	8, 71, 89
LANDIS	8	LAUCHLISON	21
LANDRETH	5, 12, 75	LAUDEN	3, 45, 63
LANDSBOROUGH	49	LAUDER	12, 63, 75
LANDSBURG	36	LAUGHHEAD	83
LANDSBURGH	21, 49, 71	LAUGHHEED	83
LANG	68	LAUN	20, 60
LANGAN	20, 37, 71	LAURANCE	1, 11, 47
LANGHOM	75	LAURENCESON	28, 56, 89
LANGHOME	75	LAURIESTON	28, 56
LANGMORE	8	LAURISTON	28, 56, 88
LANGMUIR	8, 47, 50, 71	LAUTHER	20, 37, 71
LANGSIDE	37	LAVAN	3, 33, 71
LANGSTON	87	LAVER	23
LANGTON	75, 87	LAVERICK	67
LANGWELL	5	LAVERIE	23
LANGWILL	37	LAVEROCK	28, 33, 56, 67
LANIGAN	37, 50	LAVERY	23, 37, 50, 89
LANRICK	67	LAVROCK	1, 33
LANSBOROUGH	36	LAVRY	23
LAPIN	37, 50	LAWCOCK	37, 50
LAPRAKE	83	LAWDER	23, 26, 63
LAPRICK	83	LAWHEAD	83
LAPSLEY	20, 37, 71, 89	LAWLESS	3
LAPSLIE	88, 89	LAWLISS	3
LAPSLY	89	LAWN	37, 50, 71
LAPWOOD	86	LAWRANCE	1, 11
LARG	51	LAWRENSON	28, 56, 89
LARGIE	3, 47	LAWS	1, 23
LARGS	51	LAWTIE	11
LARGUE	1, 11, 51	LAYDEN	56
LARKIN	20, 36, 37, 56	LAYRICK	33
LARSON	44	LAYTON	3, 48, 67
LART	56	LEA	26, 49, 50
LASSWADE	87	LEABURN	23
LATHAM	8, 37, 67	LEAD	89
LATTA	8, 20, 78, 71	LEADBETTER	20, 32, 56, 67
LATTER	44	LEADBITTER	26, 28, 56

SURNAME	DISTRICT	SURNAME	DISTRICT
LEADHOUSE	1	LEKEY	77
LEADINGHAM	3, 11, 47	LEMAN	47, 58, 71
LEAL	1, 11, 58, 63	LEMPITLAW	75
LEALL	58	LENIE	3, 23, 56
LEAR	26, 28, 56	LENY	21, 89
LEARD	87	LENZIES	83
LEARMOUTH	3	LEON	44
LEASON	44	LERMENT	89
LEATER	11, 37, 50	LERMON	67, 89
LEAVER	23	LERMONTH	75, 89
LEAVETT	85	LERMOUR	37, 50
LEAVITT	85	LERRICK	33
LEDDERBURROW	5	LESSELLS	28, 33, 56
LEDDINGHAM	1, 11	LESSER	JACOBITE, 1746, AM
LEDGATE	12, 56	LESSLES	1, 33
LEDGERWOOD	87	LESTEN	87
LEDINGHAM	1, 11	LETCH	33, 67, 71
LEDWICH	87	LETHAM	20, 37, 50, 87
LEDWITH	3, 23	LETHEM	87
LEDYER	75	LETHEN	33
LEE	23, 71, 77, 80	LETTERS	28, 37, 50
LEECHMAN	26, 48, 50	LETTICE	23
LEEDLE	75	LETTRICK	83
LEEK	8	LEUCHARTS	33
LEETIAN	33	LEURG	36
LEGAT	11, 56, 71	LEVENS	33
LEGERWOOD	1, 12, 75	LEVERICK	67
LEGG	1, 11, 36, 47, 87	LEVERUCK	67
LEGGAT	11, 50, 71, 89	LEVESTON	DUNBAR, 1650, AM
LEGGATE	37, 50, 71	LEVIE	1, 3
LEGGE	1, 11, 36, 87	LEVY	26, 37, 50
LEGGET	28, 47, 67, 89	LEWARS	8, 36, 50
LEGGETE	89	LEWISTON	DUNBAR, 1650, AM
LEICESTER	23	LEYBURN	75
LEICHMAN	33, 67, 89	LEYDEN	5, 20, 75, 87
LEIPER	47, 50, 71	LEYDON	50, 75
LEISTER	1, 28	LEYE	36
LEITHAM	28, 46, 56	LIBBERTON	87
LEITHEAD	12, 75, 77, 87	LIBERTON	12, 28, 75, 87
LEITHEID	12	LICHTIE	87
LEITHHEAD	21, 37, 75	LICHTY	87

SURNAME	DISTRICT	SURNAME	DISTRICT
LICKLIE	1, 3	LINEN	83
LICKLY	1	LINEY	3
LICKPRIVICK	37	LINIE	3
LIDDERDALE	17, 21, 49	LINING	83
LIDDERSDALE	31, 36	LINKLATER	1, 67, 89
LIDDESS	31	LINKSTON	28, 56, 88
LIDDIE	87	LINLAY	11
LIDDY	87	LINLIE	3
LIDGATE	12, 26, 28	LINLY	3
LIESK	15	LINN	8, 24, 36, 48, 50, 88
LIETH	15, 67, 86	LINNARD	37, 50, 67
LIGERTWOOD	1, 47	LINNAY	67
LIGGAT	89	LINNE	37, 50, 89
LIGHBODY	37, 50	LINNEN	21, 28, 49
LIGHT	37	LINSAY	37, 50, 89
LIGHTBODY	50, 67, 83, 89	LINSTER	8, 37, 88
LIGHTNING	34	LINTONS	75
LIGHTON	1, 3, 47	LINTRON	75
LIGHTOWER	86	LINWOOD	68
LIKELY	1, 3, 23	LIPP	1
LIKLY	1	LIPPOCK	44
LILBOURNE	(NFI) 1679, AM	LIPPOK	44
LILBURN	1, 33, 48, 67	LIPTON	37
LILBURNE	48, 63, 77	LISTER	21, 33, 48
LILIBURN	1	LISTON	28, 32, 56, 88
LILLBURN	33, 48, 67	LITHGOW	23, 32, 50, 67
LILLEY	12, 37, 50	LITSER	56
LILLICO	75, 77	LITSTER	26, 33, 67, 77
LILLIE	1, 12, 75	LITTLEJOHN	1, 37, 44, 48
LILLIES	28, 75, 77	LITTLESON	5
LILLY	12, 33, 75	LITTLEWOOD	8, 37, 89
LILY	50	LIVER	5, 37, 50
LIMBURNER	50	LIVIE	1, 3, 23
LIMEBURNER	8, 37	LIVISTON	3, 71, 75
LIN	12, 21, 89	LIVY	3, 37, 50
LINAY	67	LIZARS	28, 56, 75, 88
LINCH	20, 23, 89	LLOYD	28, 33, 56
LINCOLN	44	LOAN	36, 49, 71, 89
LINDESAY	28, 33, 56	LOANE	36
LINDLEY	3	LOCH	12, 56, 87, 88
LINDON	3	LOCHART	8, 37, 89

SURNAME	DISTRICT	SURNAME	DISTRICT
LOCHEAD	8, 17, 71	LOTHIAN	12, 48, 77, 87
LOCHHEAD	14, 37, 71, 80	LOUDAN	8, 12, 75
LOCHHEED	83	LOUGH	12, 36, 75, 77
LOCHMILLER	5	LOUGHMILLER	8
LOCHRAIN	8, 21	LOUMIS	83
LOCHREY	50	LOUNAN	3
LOCHRIE	23, 49, 71, 89	LOUR	3
LOCHRIN	37, 50	LOURIE	75, 77, 88
LOCHRY	23	LOUSON	3, 8, 33
LOCHTIE	33	LOUTFOOT	33
LOCK	28, 49, 56, 75	LOUTHER	17, 21, 89
LOCKE	21, 28, 49, 75	LOUTHTON	26
LOCKERBIE	8, 21, 49	LOUTIT	15, 67, 84, 89
LOCKETT	86	LOUTITT	15, 67, 84
LOCKHEAD	83	LOUTTIT	15, 67, 89
LOCKHEED	83	LOVELL	3, 20, 23, 75
LOCKWOOD	4, 17, 36, 58, 89	LOVIE	1, 11
LOCKY	3	LOWMAN	83
LOCKYER	21, 56	LOWPAR	3
LODGE	1, 71	LOWPER	3
LOMOND	83	LOWRIE	12, 47, 67
LONGER	1	LOWTH	87
LONGMURE	3, 8, 47	LOWTHER	21, 37, 50
LONGSTAFF	85	LOXTON	87
LONGTON	36	LUDDALL	75
LONNIE	28, 33, 50	LUDDELL	75
LONSDALE	17	LUDDLE	75
LOOKER	75	LUGGIE	83
LOOKUP	21, 28, 49	LUMISDEN	33, 88
LOONAN	75	LUMLEY	26, 28, 56, 83
LOOR	3	LUMLIE	83
LORAINE	28, 56	LUMLY	83
LORD	8, 33, 75	LUMMIS	83
LORIE	8, 33, 67	LUMSDALE	3, 23, 67
LORIMAR	3, 84	LUNAM	12, 26
LORIMER	3, 11, 21, 49, 84	LUNAN	1, 3, 12
LORN	20, 71, 89	LUNAR	3
LORRAIN	12, 14, 21	LUNCART	54
LORRAINE	21, 28, 56, 87	LUND	28, 33, 37, 87
LORRANE	87	LUNDEN	28, 33, 56
LORRIMER	1, 21, 50	LUNER	3

SURNAME	DISTRICT	SURNAME	DISTRICT
LUNHAM	12, 37, 49	MAC ALAVY	8
LUNN	12, 75, 77, 87	MAC ALDRIDGE	80
LUNNAN	1, 3, 12	MAC ALENEY	36
LURG	36	MAC ALLORUM	36
LURIE	11, 49, 71	MAC ALLY	8, 21, 37
LUTE	1, 20	MAC ALORUM	36
LUTIT	37, 50, 89	MAC ALULGHLIN	68
LYAL	11, 12, 26	MAC ALVENY	68
LYBURN	36	MAC ANANW	68
LYDER	1, 5, 56, 75	MAC ANASPIE	67
LYLES	28, 56, 89	MAC ANASPY	5, 67
LYNAN	58	MAC ANCH	8, 67
LYNCH	20, 23, 88	MAC ANDLES	36
LYSARS	75	MAC ANDLESS	36
LYSTER	37, 50	MAC ANDO	67
LYTE	37	MAC ANEA	68
MABEN	12, 49, 89	MAC ANEUA	68
MABERRY	50, 89	MAC ANEUAY	68
MABIN	28, 36, 49, 56	MAC ANISTAN	5
MABON	12, 36, 75, 77	MAC ANLESS	36
MAC ABE	37, 88, 89	MAC ANLIS	36
MAC ABERIE	67	MAC ANLISS	36
MAC ABERY	67	MAC ANNA	37, 71, 88
MAC ABNEY	68	MAC ANNANY	36
MAC ABRAHAM	67	MAC ANNEY	36
MAC ACHANNEY	5	MAC ANOY	87
MAC ACHEENY	5	MAC ANULLA	36
MAC ACY	8	MAC ARACHER	37, 50, 71
MAC ADOO	36	MAC ARDALE	36
MAC ADOOS	36	MAC ARDELL	36
MAC ADORIE	8	MAC ARDIE	67
MAC ADORY	8	MAC ARDILL	36
MAC ADOU	36	MAC ARDLE	1, 20, 23, 36
MAC ADOW	36	MAC AREAVY	36
MAC AFFER	5, 71	MAC ARGH	36
MAC AFFERTY	8, 28, 71	MAC ARGHER	36
MAC AIL	50, 67	MAC ARGLE	36
MAC AINCH	20, 37, 50	MAC ARRAN	68
MAC ALANENY	68	MAC ARVER	36
MAC ALASTER	5, 15, 21	MAC ARVIE	36
MAC ALAVEY	8	MAC ASKELL	45, 75

SURNAME	DISTRICT	SURNAME	DISTRICT
MAC ASKIL	15, 45, 75	MAC BLACKIE	36
MAC ASPEN	36	MAC BLACKY	36
MAC ASPUN	36	MAC BLAINE	36
MAC ASSER	36	MAC BLAININE	36
MAC ASTNEY	8, 36	MAC BLANE	8, 36, 37, 50
MAC ASTOCKER	36	MAC BLAREN	67
MAC ASWINNING	68	MAC BRACADAIR	38
MAC ATANGAY	68	MAC BRACHTER	38
MAC ATASNEY	37	MAC BRAIRDY	37, 50
MAC ATE	36	MAC BRECK	67
MAC ATEE	36	MAC BRIEN	3, 23, 88
MAC ATEMNEY	68	MAC BRIER	36
MAC ATHIE	33, 48, 67	MAC BROOKS	67
MAC AUALY	37, 50	MAC BROOM	3, 8, 23
MAC AUCHTRIE	37, 50	MAC BRYAR	36
MAC AUGHER	36	MAC BURNEY	21, 37, 50
MAC AUGHTRIE	8, 44	MAC BURNIE	21, 49, 77
MAC AUGHTRY	44	MAC CABERIE	67
MAC AULY	37, 67, 88	MAC CABERY	67
MAC AUSLAND	5, 20, 71	MAC CADIE	89
MAC AUSLANE	20, 56, 71	MAC CAFFRAY	23, 37, 50
MAC AUTRIE	44	MAC CAGHERTIE	87
MAC AUTRY	44	MAC CAGHERTY	87
MAC AVENNIE	68	MAC CAIGNIE	67
MAC AVERIE	67	MAC CAIGNY	67
MAC AVERY	67	MAC CAIL	5, 37, 88
MAC AVINEY	36	MAC CAILL	5 21, 67
MAC AVINUE	25	MAC CAIRDLE	8
MAC AVINY	36	MAC CAIRN	20, 37, 89
MAC AVOE	68	MAC CAIRNEY	37, 50
MAC BADE	36	MAC CALIDEN	84
MAC BAIDE	36	MAC CALINDEN	WORCESTER, 1652, AM
MAC BARNET	37, 45, 75	MAC CALKEN	5
MAC BAYDGE	36	MAC CALKIN	5
MAC BECK	36	MAC CALLACHIE	23
MAC BEIDE	36	MAC CALLACHY	23
MAC BENNET	75	MAC CALLOW	21, 89
MAC BENNETT	75	MAC CALSTON	75
MAC BEY	11, 47, 58	MAC CAMNACK	16
MAC BILE	36	MAC CANASPIE	8
MAC BILES	36	MAC CANASPY	8

SURNAME	DISTRICT	SURNAME	DISTRICT
MAC CANCH	36	MAC CASSLESS	8
MAC CANCHY	36	MAC CASTED	1
MAC CANDEIL	36	MAC CASTER	1
MAC CANDEILS	36	MAC CASTOR	1
MAC CANDIE	28, 33, 75	MAC CATCHIE	16
MAC CANDLISH	8, 36, 49, 89	MAC CATCHY	16
MAC CANKIE	33	MAC CATE	36
MAC CANLIES	36	MAC CATHIE	1, 33
MAC CANQUELL	87	MAC CATHY	28, 56
MAC CANSKIE	87	MAC CAUGHIE	21, 49, 89
MAC CANSKY	87	MAC CAUGHNEY	68
MAC CANT	37, 50, 67	MAC CAUGHTER	36
MAC CARA	8, 56, 89	MAC CAUGHTREY	44
MAC CARBLE	36	MAC CAUGHTRY	44
MAC CARDALE	28, 56	MAC CAULL	49, 67, 89
MAC CARDEL	36	MAC CAUSLAND	28, 37, 50
MAC CARDELL	36	MAC CAVIT	36
MAC CARDEN	68	MAC CAVITT	36
MAC CARDLE	1, 8, 36	MAC CAWBER	5
MAC CARG	36	MAC CAWISH	5
MAC CARGAR	36	MAC CAYLEY	36
MAC CARGH	36	MAC CELIE	36
MAC CARGILL	67	MAC CELIY	36
MAC CARGO	8, 36, 89	MAC CESS	68
MAC CARICK	16	MAC CHANBLE	8
MAC CARLEY	8, 71, 89	MAC CHANBLY	8
MAC CARNOCHAN	36	MAC CHAPMAN	67
MAC CARRICK	8, 16, 89	MAC CHARGUE	36
MAC CARRIG	16	MAC CHARLARTIE	ARGYLL'S REBELLION, 1685, AM
MAC CARRISON	36		
MAC CARROLL	37, 50	MAC CHISHOLM	COVENANTER, 1684, AM
MAC CARSIE	3	MAC CHORD	36
MAC CARSY	3	MAC CHRYSTAL	3, 37, 50
MAC CARTELL	36	MAC CHURCH	36
MAC CARTENEY	1, 21, 71	MAC CHURG	36
MAC CARTLE	36	MAC CIMLIN	36
MAC CASHNIE	23	MAC CIMLON	36
MAC CASHNY	23	MAC CLACHRIE	36
MAC CASKELL	45, 71, 75	MAC CLAFERTIE	36
MAC CASLESS	8	MAC CLAFERTY	36
MAC CASSEY	1	MAC CLAMMA	36

SURNAME	DISTRICT	SURNAME	DISTRICT
MAC CLANACHAN	8	MAC CLOWY	5
MAC CLANSBURG	87	MAC CLUHAN	5
MAC CLANSBURGH	87	MAC CLUMG	36
MAC CLASER	JACOBITE, 1716, AM	MAC CLUMPHA	28, 36, 56, 89
MAC CLATCHER	36	MAC CLUN	7
MAC CLATCHET	16	MAC CLUNE	8, 21, 49
MAC CLATCHIE	8, 16, 21, 49, 68	MAC CLUNG	8, 36, 71
MAC CLATCHY	16, 68	MAC CLURG	(NFI) 1684, AM
MAC CLAUCHIE	36	MAC COACH	16
MAC CLAVERTIE	68	MAC COATS	16
MAC CLAVERTY	68	MAC COBIUS	5
MAC CLAWSON	67	MAC COE	ROYALIST, 1652, AM
MAC CLEAKERIE	87	MAC COIK	7
MAC CLEAKERY	87	MAC COLASH	44
MAC CLEAN	8, 58, 89	MAC COLD	8, 71, 89
MAC CLEANE	28, 56, 89	MAC COLGAN	8, 20, 37, 71
MAC CLEERY	67	MAC COLGANE	8
MAC CLEIKERAYE	(NFI) 1679, AM	MAC COLGIN	8
MAC CLELAND	26, 28, 49	MAC COLGINE	8
MAC CLENAGHAN	36, 68	MAC COLLA	36
MAC CLENAGHEN	68	MAC COLTON	36
MAC CLENAHAN	36	MAC COLVIN	75
MAC CLENNAN	1, 8	MAC COLVINE	75
MAC CLENTEN	36	MAC COMBS	20, 37, 71
MAC CLENTON	36	MAC COME	WORCESTER, 1652, AM
MAC CLEOD	37, 75, 88	MAC COMINSKIE	87
MAC CLETCHIE	8	MAC COMISKIE	87
MAC CLINGAN	36	MAC COMISTRIE	36
MAC CLINGEN	36	MAC COMISTRY	36
MAC CLOREY	36	MAC CONACHAR	5, 89
MAC CLORGAN	36	MAC CONACHY	5, 11, 14
MAC CLORIE	36	MAC CONASTER	36
MAC CLORY	36	MAC CONAWAY	44
MAC CLOUD	21, 49, 89	MAC CONAY	44
MAC CLOUGHNEY	37	MAC CONDOCHIE	58, 67
MAC CLOUGHRIE	16	MAC CONDOO	67
MAC CLOUGHRY	16	MAC CONDUIBH	67
MAC CLOUNIE	36	MAC CONE	WORCESTER, 1652, AM
MAC CLOUNY	36	MAC CONELL	37, 50, 89
MAC CLOUTHEN	JACOBITE, 1747, AM	MAC CONISTER	36
MAC CLOWIE	5	MAC CONNAL	21, 49, 89

SURNAME	DISTRICT	SURNAME	DISTRICT
MAC CONNAN	20, 21, 23	MAC COWIN	JACOBITE, 1747, AM
MAC CONNEL	8, 49, 89	MAC COWNIE	8, 37, 50
MAC CONNICH	41	MAC CRAB	1
MAC CONNICK	41	MAC CRABBIE	28, 56
MAC CONNOCHY	8, 14, 71	MAC CRACKET	12
MAC CONOCHY	5, 14, 23	MAC CRACKON	49
MAC CONSER	5	MAC CRAFT	36
MAC CONVIL	23, 37, 50	MAC CRAGG	1
MAC CONVILLE	28, 49, 88	MAC CRAING	44
MAC CORBEY	5	MAC CRAKEN	17, 21, 49
MAC CORGRAY	44	MAC CRANER	5
MAC CORGREY	44	MAC CRANOR	5
MAC CORKADALE	(NFI) 1685, AM	MAC CRAVEN	36
MAC CORKDALE	(NFI) 1685, AM	MAC CRAVENS	36
MAC CORMIC	45, 50, 89	MAC CRAVEY	36
MAC COROLOGUE	68	MAC CRAVIE	36
MAC CORQUDALE	5, 20, 71	MAC CRAVIEE	36
MAC CORQUODLE	5	MAC CRAVY	36
MAC CORRAL	16	MAC CREABY	68
MAC CORRALL	16	MAC CREADIE	8, 36, 49, 89
MAC CORTIL	68	MAC CREADY	8, 36, 37, 89
MAC CORVIE	5	MAC CREANOR	5, 36
MAC CORVY	5	MAC CREARY	8, 21, 37, 67
MAC CORWIS	5	MAC CREDDAN	36
MAC COSCHRIE	36	MAC CREDDIE	8, 49, 89
MAC COSKER	37	MAC CREDIE	8, 36, 49, 89
MAC COSKERRIE	36	MAC CREDY	36
MAC COSKERY	36	MAC CREEDIE	8, 36, 37, 50
MAC COSKRIE	49, 89	MAC CREEDY	36
MAC COUAT	71, 89	MAC CREEK	75
MAC COULESKIE	5	MAC CREEKIE	87
MAC COULESKY	5	MAC CREEKY	87
MAC COURT	3, 16, 23, 89	MAC CRICKARD	1
MAC COURTEREY	36	MAC CRICKART	1
MAC COURTIE	21, 47, 49	MAC CRICKETT	1
MAC COURTNEY	36, 37, 50, 89	MAC CRIDDY	36
MAC COURTUEY	36	MAC CRIERICK	67
MAC COURTUIE	THIEF, 1770, AM	MAC CRIRICK	36
MAC COURTY	20, 21, 49	MAC CRIRRICK	36
MAC COWAT	36	MAC CROCKET	89
MAC COWATT	36	MAC CROCKETT	89

SURNAME	DISTRICT	SURNAME	DISTRICT
MAC CRODDAN	23	MAC CURM	1
MAC CRODDEN	23	MAC DANELL	JACOBITE, 1716, AM
MAC CRODDIE	36	MAC DARRAN	JACOBITE, 1716, AM
MAC CRODDY	36	MAC DERMONT	1, 8, 23
MAC CRODEN	23	MAC DERMOT	37, 47, 49
MAC CROFT	36	MAC DICHMAYE	(NFI) 1679, AM
MAC CROHAN	23, 68	MAC DICKMIE	87
MAC CRON	21, 36, 37, 88	MAC DICKMY	87
MAC CRONE	8, 21, 36, 67	MAC DIER	23
MAC CROREY	37, 50, 89	MAC DILLIDA	1
MAC CRORIE	8, 28, 56	MAC DILLIDAF	1
MAC CROSKIE	84	MAC DINE	36
MAC CROSKRIE	36	MAC DINES	36
MAC CROSTIE	17, 28, 56, 84	MAC DIRMAID	37, 45, 50
MAC CROSTY	84	MAC DIVOT	1, 37, 71
MAC CRUAR	87	MAC DOLAN	37
MAC CRUDDEN	23	MAC DOLAND	68
MAC CRUSKER	23	MAC DONACH	37, 50
MAC CRYSTAL	10	MAC DONAL	8, 37, 89
MAC CRYSTALL	10	MAC DONALL	21, 75, 89
MAC CUBBEN	8, 21, 37	MAC DONART	36
MAC CUEAN	COVENANTER, 1685, AM	MAC DOO	36
MAC CUIG	28, 56	MAC DOOR	44
MAC CUILLAN	15	MAC DORE	44
MAC CULASKIE	5	MAC DORFF	1
MAC CULASKY	5	MAC DORR	44
MAC CULLON	JACOBITE, 1716, AM	MAC DORRAN	75
MAC CULLONIE	44	MAC DORREN	75
MAC CULLONY	44	MAC DORTAN	8
MAC CULLOY	36	MAC DORTIN	8
MAC CULLUCH	71	MAC DORTON	JACOBITE, 1716, AM
MAC CULLUM	5, 67, 69	MAC DOUGALD	5, 14, 45
MAC CUNEO	7	MAC DOUNIE	87
MAC CUNNIE	36	MAC DOUNY	87
MAC CUNNY	36	MAC DOVE	37, 50, 77
MAC CUR	87	MAC DOWEL	8, 37, 50
MAC CURACH	11, 28, 56	MAC DOWNEY	87
MAC CUREITH	(NFI) 1685, AM	MAC DOWNIE	87
MAC CURIN	5	MAC DUE	36
MAC CURIN	5	MAC DUGALL	5, 11, 86
MAC CURM	1	MAC DUNE	8

SURNAME	DISTRICT	SURNAME	DISTRICT
MAC DUNN	8	MAC ENANEY	68
MAC DYER	23	MAC ENDRICK	56
MAC DYRE	1	MAC ENHILL	23
MAC E	56	MAC ENTAFFER	1
MAC EACHRAN	5, 37, 75	MAC EOROY	36
MAC EANOR	73	MAC EREATY	37
MAC EARLICH	75	MAC ERNOCH	5
MAC EDWARD	11, 45, 63	MAC ERNOK	5
MAC ELATIN	36	MAC EVEN	36
MAC ELATINE	36	MAC FADZEN	8, 26, 89
MAC ELAVEY	36	MAC FAGAN	36, 49
MAC ELENEY	68	MAC FAGEN	36
MAC ELENIE	87	MAC FAGGAN	36
MAC ELENNIE	87	MAC FAGGEN	36
MAC ELENNY	87	MAC FALLAN	89
MAC ELENY	87	MAC FARLINE	23, 48, 89
MAC ELGAY	68	MAC FARSON	WORCESTER, 1652, AM
MAC ELHAE	36	MAC FAUN	36
MAC ELHILL	37, 68	MAC FAWN	36
MAC ELHINNRY	37	MAC FEARGHUIS	JACOBITE, 1747, AM
MAC ELHOLM	68	MAC FEATE	20
MAC ELHONE	37	MAC FEDRIES	36
MAC ELHUTTEN	68	MAC FEELY	28, 37, 50
MAC ELHUTTON	68	MAC FEGAN	36
MAC ELLIGER	7	MAC FEGANS	36
MAC ELLIICHER	7	MAC FEGGAN	21, 36, 49
MAC ELMEL	37	MAC FEGGANS	36
MAC ELNAY	87	MAC FEIGAN	5
MAC ELNEA	87	MAC FEIGANS	5
MAC ELNEY	68, 87	MAC FEIGGAN	5
MAC ELNIE	87	MAC FEIGGANS	5
MAC ELNY	87	MAC FELL	20, 28, 56
MAC ELORY	36	MAC FEN	5
MAC ELQUHAM	37	MAC FENN	5
MAC ELSTALKER	8	MAC FERN	36
MAC ELVOGUE	37, 44, 68	MAC FERRAN	44, 36
MAC ELVRIDE	5	MAC FERREN	44, 36
MAC EMLIN	7	MAC FERRIAN	44
MAC EMLINE	7	MAC FERRIN	44
MAC EMLINN	7	MAC FERRY	44
MAC EMLINNE	7	MAC FERY	44

SURNAME	DISTRICT	SURNAME	DISTRICT
MAC FIGAN	5	MAC GARDLE	36
MAC FIGANS	5	MAC GARERY	36
MAC FIGGAN	5	MAC GARIGLE	68
MAC FIGGANS	5	MAC GARITY	87
MAC FIGGIN	36	MAC GARR	36
MAC FIGGINS	36	MAC GARRACH	8, 89
MAC FIGIN	36	MAC GARRACHAN	36
MAC FIGINS	36	MAC GARRAHAN	36
MAC FILANE	5	MAC GARRELL	36
MAC FILLANS	84	MAC GARRETY	37, 50
MAC FILLECHAIR	44	MAC GARRIE	37, 81, 89
MAC FILLENS	84	MAC GARRITY	37, 68, 71, 87, 89
MAC FLIKER	8	MAC GARROCH	8, 68
MAC FOD	23	MAC GARRVEY	36
MAC FOIL	5	MAC GARTLAND	68
MAC FOLAN	84	MAC GARTLIN	87
MAC FOLER	8	MAC GARTLINE	87
MAC FOLLAN	84	MAC GARTY	37, 50
MAC FOLLEY	8	MAC GARVA	8, 36, 49, 89
MAC FONN	36	MAC GARVAH	8, 36
MAC FORD	23	MAC GARVE	36
MAC FOYLE	5	MAC GARVEY	36
MAC FREDERICK	37	MAC GARVIE	8, 36, 71, 89
MAC FREDEROCK	37	MAC GARVIN	36
MAC FRUCTER	54	MAC GARVOCK	3
MAC FRUCTOR	54	MAC GARVY	36
MAC FRY	23	MAC GATHAN	68
MAC FRYE	23	MAC GATLIN	87
MAC GAAN	8, 37, 50	MAC GATLINE	87
MAC GABOCK	3	MAC GAUCHIE	21, 33, 71
MAC GACHIN	8	MAC GAUGHIE	28, 49, 56
MAC GAFFERTY	71, 89	MAC GAVIGAN	87
MAC GAFFIGAN	68	MAC GAVIN	3, 8, 23
MAC GAFFNEY	37	MAC GAVROCK	87
MAC GAHIE	37, 50	MAC GEACHEY	5, 37, 50
MAC GAIN	37	MAC GEER	36
MAC GALLAGHY	68	MAC GEGGEN	23
MAC GAN	33, 50, 71	MAC GEGGIN	23
MAC GANN	8, 71	MAC GENLY	21
MAC GARAVA	36	MAC GENN	37
MAC GARAVAH	36	MAC GENNITY	37

SURNAME	DISTRICT	SURNAME	DISTRICT
MAC GENSIE	23	MAC GIMPSIE	36
MAC GENSY	23	MAC GIMPSY	36
MAC GEOCH	36, 49, 71, 89	MAC GIMSIE	36
MAC GEOGEGHAN	23	MAC GINLAY	37, 50, 89
MAC GEOGHIE	23	MAC GINN	23, 71, 89
MAC GEOGHY	23	MAC GINNIES	8, 20, 49
MAC GEOUGH	8, 37, 50	MAC GINTIE	37
MAC GERR	36	MAC GINTY	37, 50, 71
MAC GERREY	37, 50	MAC GIRK	83
MAC GERRY	5, 37, 50	MAC GIRR	36, 49, 71, 89
MAC GERVEY	36	MAC GIURK	83
MAC GETIGAN	3	MAC GIVEN	23, 88, 89
MAC GETTIGAN	3	MAC GIVER	50, 56, 89
MAC GHIN	37	MAC GLADERIE	87
MAC GIBNEY	3, 23, 89	MAC GLADERY	87
MAC GIE	37, 50, 71	MAC GLADIGAN	37
MAC GIFF	36	MAC GLADREY	87
MAC GIFFE	36	MAC GLADRIE	21, 50, 67, 87
MAC GIL	20, 89	MAC GLADRIGAN	37
MAC GILGLASS	42	MAC GLADRY	87
MAC GILGUNN	36	MAC GLAME	37
MAC GILLAN	20, 67, 75	MAC GLAMIE	37
MAC GILLEGLASS	54	MAC GLAMMIE	37
MAC GILLEVERAY	JACOBITE, PRESTON, 1716, AM	MAC GLATCHIE	16
		MAC GLATCHY	16
MAC GILLEVEREY	JACOBITE, PRESTON, 1716, AM	MAC GLATHERIE	87
		MAC GLATHERY	87
MAC GILLEWIE	67	MAC GLATIN	36
MAC GILLIARG	8	MAC GLATINE	36
MAC GILLICH	ARGYLL'S REBELLION, 1685, AM	MAC GLEN	36
		MAC GLENN	36
MAC GILLIEWIE	67	MAC GLENNS	36
MAC GILLIS	44	MAC GLENS	36
MAC GILLIVERAY	JACOBITE, PRESTON, 1716, AM	MAC GLIMACHIE	87
		MAC GLIMACHY	87
MAC GILLRAE	56	MAC GLINCHEY	37, 50, 71
MAC GILNEW	74	MAC GLINCHIE	37
MAC GILRA	8	MAC GLINCHY	23, 37, 50
MAC GILRAY	8	MAC GLINN	37, 50, 71
MAC GILREY	8	MAC GLOAN	37, 50, 71
MAC GILRIE	8	MAC GLOANE	50
MAC GILTON	16		

SURNAME	DISTRICT	SURNAME	DISTRICT
MAC GLODRICK	23	MAC GOWGAN	52
MAC GLOGAN	68	MAC GOWIE	50
MAC GLOHAN	23	MAC GOWN	20, 37, 71
MAC GLOHN	16	MAC GRADDIE	68
MAC GLOHON	16	MAC GRADE	68
MAC GLOM	36	MAC GRADER	84
MAC GLOMAGLE	68	MAC GRADEY	36
MAC GLON	36	MAC GRAFFE	36
MAC GLONE	1, 8, 36, 37	MAC GRAFFEY	36
MAC GLOUN	36	MAC GRALE	37, 50
MAC GLOWN	36	MAC GRANAHAN	87
MAC GLUICHEY	16	MAC GREADY	36
MAC GLUMPHY	36	MAC GREEDIE	36
MAC GLYN	36	MAC GREEDY	36
MAC GLYNN	36	MAC GREEN	36
MAC GLYNNS	36	MAC GREENE	36
MAC GLYNS	36	MAC GREESKIN	87
MAC GOLDRICK	37, 87	MAC GREESKINE	87
MAC GOLERICK	23	MAC GRESKIN	37
MAC GOLVIN	75	MAC GROGAR	68
MAC GOLVINE	75	MAC GROGARTY	68
MAC GONEGAL	37, 50, 71	MAC GROSSAN	36
MAC GONIGAL	3, 23, 71	MAC GUARRIA	68
MAC GONIGE	68	MAC GUCKIN	37, 50, 71
MAC GONIGILL	86	MAC GUFFOG	21, 49, 89
MAC GONNIGAL	37, 50	MAC GUFFOY	49, 89
MAC GOODWIN	89	MAC GUGIN	36
MAC GOOTRAY	44	MAC GUIDWIN	89
MAC GORAU	68	MAC GUILLONE	36
MAC GORLICK	36	MAC GUINNIETY	37
MAC GORMAN	8	MAC GUINNITY	37
MAC GOUCHTRAY	8	MAC GUIRK	3, 23, 71, 80
MAC GOUGHTRIE	8	MAC GUIRN	68
MAC GOUGHTRY	8	MAC GULORICK	68
MAC GOUIRK	83	MAC GUNNIGAL	68
MAC GOULDRICK	37	MAC GUNNIGLE	68
MAC GOURLICK	68	MAC GUNNION	36
MAC GOVAN	20, 37, 50	MAC GUNNON	36
MAC GOVANEY	37	MAC GUR	36
MAC GOVARN	68	MAC GURAN	68
MAC GOVERN	23, 28, 56	MAC GURK	37, 49, 50, 83

SURNAME	DISTRICT	SURNAME	DISTRICT
MAC GURKIN	36	MAC ILBREED	5
MAC GURN	84, 68	MAC ILBRYDE	ARGYLL'S REBELLION, 1685, AM
MAC GURNEE	84		
MAC GURNIE	84	MAC ILCACHEW	54
MAC GURNIGAN	68	MAC ILCHALLUM	67
MAC GURNY	84	MAC ILCHERE	7
MAC HACKIE	68	MAC ILCHERIE	7
MAC HACKY	68	MAC ILDEEN	37
MAC HACNEY	68	MAC ILGORM	37, 68
MAC HAGH	68	MAC ILHAGGA	87
MAC HALLUM	8, 49, 89	MAC ILHAGGER	68
MAC HAN	47, 50, 89	MAC ILHARDY	87
MAC HANE	71	MAC ILHARGA	87
MAC HAR	1, 3, 89	MAC ILHARGAH	87
MAC HARG	8, 36, 49, 89	MAC ILHARGE	87
MAC HARGUE	36	MAC ILHARGEY	87
MAC HARR	1	MAC ILHARGIE	87
MAC HATTIE	1, 11, 58	MAC ILHAUGH	36
MAC HAYLER	36	MAC ILHENNY	37, 50
MAC HELL	74	MAC ILHILL	36
MAC HER	7	MAC ILHINNY	68
MAC HERIOD	3	MAC ILHINY	68
MAC HERR	7	MAC ILHON	36, 37
MAC HIE	1, 11, 33	MAC ILHONE	8, 37, 50
MAC HINTON	7	MAC ILHONY	36, 37
MAC HIR	3, 49	MAC ILKEARNY	67
MAC HOLLAM	75	MAC ILLIGLAS	5
MAC HONAGAN	5	MAC ILLIP	50
MAC HUDRIE	83	MAC ILMAIL	8, 37, 50
MAC HUDRY	83	MAC ILMOON	ARGYLL'S REBELLION, 1685, AM
MAC HUG	87		
MAC HURG	36	MAC ILMOYL	87
MAC HUTCHEON	8, 20, 49	MAC ILNAY	87
MAC HUTCHIN	28, 56	MAC ILNEW	5
MAC HUTCHISON	8, 71, 89	MAC ILONEY	83
MAC HUTCHON	20, 28, 49	MAC ILPHERSON	21, 36
MAC HWOIL	45	MAC ILQUHAM	20, 37, 50
MAC ICHAN	6	MAC ILROW	34
MAC IF	36	MAC ILSHALLUM	ARGYLL'S REBELLION, 1685, AM
MAC IFF	36		
MAC ILBOWIE	38	MAC ILUDE	37
		MAC ILVAY	(NFI) 1684, AM

SURNAME	DISTRICT	SURNAME	DISTRICT
MAC ILVERNOCH	5	MAC JARVIS	89
MAC ILVERNOT	5	MAC JASPAR	44
MAC ILVERRAN	5	MAC JASPER	44
MAC ILVONE	73	MAC JEDS	75
MAC ILVOY	36	MAC JENKIN	83
MAC ILVRIDE	28, 56, 67	MAC JENKINS	83
MAC ILVRONE	34	MAC JERROW	8, 36
MAC ILWHAM	89	MAC JILTON	16
MAC ILWRAITH	8, 71, 89	MAC JIMPSEY	36
MAC ILWRICK	8, 71, 89	MAC JIMSEY	36
MAC INAIRNE	36	MAC JIMSIE	36
MAC INALL	25	MAC JOLLY	8
MAC INLIER	JACOBITE, PRESTON, 1716, AM	MAC JORROW	68
		MAC JOS	33
MAC INLUDE	37	MAC JOSS	33
MAC INNA	49	MAC JULTON	16
MAC INNEY	37, 50, 71	MAC K	12, 26, 77
MAC INNON	3, 37, 88	MAC KAINE	ROYALIST, WORCESTER, 1652, AM
MAC INNY	JACOBITE, 1747, AM		
MAC INRIVER	5	MAC KAIRNE	ARGYLL'S REBELLION, 1685, AM
MAC INSTER	36		
MAC INSTRAY	36	MAC KALE	8
MAC INSTREY	36	MAC KANDY	2
MAC INTAGGART	5, 14, 37	MAC KANNA	8, 20, 37
MAC INTIRE	8, 17, 23	MAC KARDELL	16
MAC INTULTY	68	MAC KAREN	67
MAC INULTIE	87	MAC KARGE	36
MAC INULTY	87	MAC KARRICK	16
MAC INVICH	68	MAC KARTNEY	21, 50, 58
MAC INVICK	68	MAC KASH	45, 67, 75
MAC INVILL	7	MAC KAVEECH	37
MAC INWILL	7	MAC KEANA	36
MAC IRONSIDE	1	MAC KEAND	21, 49, 89
MAC ISAAK	ARGYLL'S REBELLION, 1685, AM	MAC KEANE	37, 50
		MAC KEATING	37
MAC ISACK	17, 33, 67	MAC KEBEN	5
MAC IVAR	11, 15, 86	MAC KECHAN	5, 8, 71
MAC IWANRY	68	MAC KEECH	5
MAC JANET	8, 36, 49, 89	MAC KEELS	JACOBITE, 1716, AM
MAC JANETT	36	MAC KEEN	1, 21, 49
MAC JANNET	8, 36, 49, 89	MAC KEGNEY	68

SURNAME	DISTRICT	SURNAME	DISTRICT
MAC KEICH	5, 14, 67	MAC KEUR	28, 49, 56
MAC KEICHAN	67	MAC KHELLIN	WORCESTER, 1651, AM
MAC KEIG	5, 37, 50	MAC KICHEN	20, 71
MAC KEIGH	89	MAC KIDD	45, 58
MAC KELBIE	36	MAC KIDDIE	23, 75, 77
MAC KELBY	36	MAC KIECH	8, 67 89
MAC KELDIN	37	MAC KILBRIDE	25, 37
MAC KELLEN	20, 37, 50	MAC KILBRUDE	25
MAC KELLIGETT	8	MAC KILL	8, 21, 49
MAC KELLO	REBELLION, 1685, AM	MAC KILLAGAN	1
MAC KELLOR	5, 28, 37	MAC KILLAR	5, 20, 71
MAC KELTON	36	MAC KILLIP	5, 45, 71
MAC KELVIN	14, 21, 71	MAC KILLIVANDICK	45
MAC KEMMIE	11, 58, 71	MAC KILLON	6
MAC KEN	1, 49, 75	MAC KILLUP	5, 49, 75
MAC KENCHIE	1, 14, 89	MAC KILREAS	8
MAC KEND	36	MAC KIN	5, 20, 49
MAC KENDALL	8	MAC KINCAIRN	85
MAC KENDLE	8	MAC KINCARDIE	33
MAC KENN	JACOBITE, 1716, AM	MAC KINCARDY	33
MAC KENNAN	45, 75, 89	MAC KINDELL	36
MAC KENNY	JACOBITE, 1716, AM	MAC KINDLE	37, 50
MAC KENSIE	45, 63, 67	MAC KINDLES	36
MAC KENTHOW	WORCESTER, 1651, AM	MAC KINDLESS	36
MAC KEOHNIE	3	MAC KING	14, 15, 75
MAC KEOHNY	3	MAC KINISTERY	37
MAC KERAGHAN	36	MAC KINISTRIE	8
MAC KERCHAN	28, 56, 71	MAC KINISTRY	8
MAC KERCHEN	5	MAC KINLY	14, 15, 23
MAC KERGO	36	MAC KINN	20, 37, 89
MAC KERIGAN	36	MAC KINNEL	21, 49, 89
MAC KERN	37, 50, 71	MAC KINNIN	5, 20, 45
MAC KERRAGHAN	36	MAC KINON	5, 45, 71
MAC KERREL	36	MAC KINSIE	45, 67, 89
MAC KERROW	8, 37, 50	MAC KINSTER	36
MAC KERRY	8, 37, 50	MAC KINSTRAY	36
MAC KERSIE	5, 33, 75	MAC KINSTRIE	36
MAC KERTNEY	8, 37, 89	MAC KINSTRY	36
MAC KESSON	67	MAC KINTON	54
MAC KETH	WORCESTER, 1651, AM	MAC KINTY	28, 56, 67
MAC KETHRICK	21	MAC KINTYRE	63, 67, 86

SURNAME	DISTRICT	SURNAME	DISTRICT
MAC KINVILL	5	MAC KUSKER	37
MAC KINVILLE	5	MAC LAGEN	3, 23, 67
MAC KINVINE	5	MAC LAIRD	87
MAC KIRBY	8	MAC LAMMEY	36
MAC KIRDLE	36	MAC LAMMIEE	36
MAC KIRRECH	5	MAC LANACHAN	8, 36, 50
MAC KIRRECK	5	MAC LANAHAN	36
MAC KIRRICH	5	MAC LANDERS	26, 67
MAC KIRRICK	16	MAC LANDRESS	67
MAC KIRROCH	5	MAC LANDSBOURGH	36
MAC KISCADDEN	35	MAC LANSBOURGH	36
MAC KISCADDIN	35	MAC LARKIN	37, 50
MAC KISON	17, 67, 89	MAC LATCHEY	8, 16
MAC KISSON	1, 67	MAC LATCHIE	8, 16, 36, 71, 89
MAC KISTON	89	MAC LATCHY	36
MAC KITCHEN	23, 56, 89	MAC LAUCHIE	36
MAC KITTING	8	MAC LAUCHLAN	49, 81, 89
MAC KLATCHIE	8	MAC LAUCHLANE	23, 37, 67
MAC KLATCHY	8	MAC LAUCHLIN	14, 47, 89
MAC KLEM	1	MAC LAUGHLAN	37, 49, 71
MAC KMILLER	8	MAC LAUGHLAND	3, 8, 67
MAC KNAUGHT	49, 89	MAC LAUGHLIN	20, 67, 71
MAC KNEW	87	MAC LAUGHTON	14, 49, 71
MAC KNIE	67, 71	MAC LAWRIE	33, 89
MAC KNITH	WORCESTER, 1651, AM	MAC LEAMAN	1, 75
MAC KNO	36	MAC LEARINS	JACOBITE, PRESTON, 1716, AM
MAC KNOE	36	MAC LEARNAN	74
MAC KNOON	36	MAC LEARNAND	74
MAC KONNACHIE	1, 3	MAC LEESBACH	67
MAC KOREST	67	MAC LEESBACK	67
MAC KORKINDALE	20, 50, 71	MAC LEITH	83
MAC KORREST	67	MAC LEMAN	1, 75, 86
MAC KOVICH	67	MAC LEMEE	68
MAC KOWIAC	67	MAC LENADEN	36
MAC KRIDE	8	MAC LENAHAN	36
MAC KRIDES	8	MAC LENAN	45, 63, 75
MAC KRIDGE	36	MAC LENNIE	50
MAC KROKAT	37	MAC LEOR	45, 75, 89
MAC KRONE	36	MAC LETCHIE	8, 12, 16, 88
MAC KTRETH	WORCESTER, 1651, AM		
MAC KUNE	21, 37, 49		

SURNAME	DISTRICT	SURNAME	DISTRICT
MAC LETCHY	8, 16	MAC MALLESS	DUNBAR, 1650, AM
MAC LEUCHLAN	36	MAC MALLY	56
MAC LEUCHLEN	36	MAC MALMURE	83
MAC LEWIN	5	MAC MANAMON	68
MAC LIESH	17, 48, 67	MAC MANAMY	36
MAC LIMONT	8, 20, 89	MAC MANN	37, 50, 89
MAC LINE	ARGYLL'S REBELLION, 1685, AM	MAC MANNY	71
		MAC MAPH	36
MAC LINKO	37	MAC MAUGH	36
MAC LINNAN	45, 75	MAC MAYBEN	36
MAC LIVE	8, 11	MAC MECKAN	37, 49, 89
MAC LOON	36	MAC MECKEN	8, 28, 89
MAC LOONE	36	MAC MECKIN	28, 56, 89
MAC LORI	36	MAC MECKINE	89
MAC LORRIE	36	MAC MECUM	16
MAC LORY	36	MAC MECUME	16
MAC LORYD	16	MAC MEEHEN	16
MAC LOSKIE	49	MAC MEEKEN	8, 28, 56
MAC LOSKY	8, 20, 71	MAC MEEKIN	16, 89
MAC LOUGHLAN	JACOBITE, PRESTON, 1716, AM	MAC MEEKINS	16
		MAC MEHENS	16
MAC LOUGHLIN	3, 23, 71	MAC MEIKAN	16
MAC LOURTANEY	36	MAC MEIKEN	16
MAC LOW	3, 23, 67	MAC MEKAN	28, 56, 89
MAC LOWTHAN	44	MAC MEKIN	16
MAC LOWTHEN	44	MAC MENEMIE	36
MAC LUE	8, 75, 89	MAC MENEMY	36
MAC LUMFA	36	MAC MENIDE	5
MAC LUMPHA	36	MAC MENIDY	5
MAC LUMPHAS	36	MAC MENIGALL	36
MAC LUSKEY	20, 37, 50	MAC MERAMIN	87
MAC LUSKY	20, 37, 88	MAC MERIT	5
MAC MABEN	16	MAC MERRIMAN	87
MAC MABY	16	MAC MICHEL	49, 71, 75
MAC MACHEN	16	MAC MICHEN	8, 88, 89
MAC MACHENN	16	MAC MICKAN	21, 49, 89
MAC MAHON	23, 37, 49	MAC MICKEN	8, 49
MAC MAHONE	20	MAC MICKING	8, 20, 81, 89
MAC MAKENS	36	MAC MILER	8
MAC MALBRIDE	83	MAC MILKEN	7, 49, 89
MAC MALLEM	DUNBAR, 1650, AM	MAC MILLAR	20, 81, 89

SURNAME	DISTRICT	SURNAME	DISTRICT
MAC MILLER	8	MAC NEILEGE	20, 37, 71
MAC MIN	8, 21, 49	MAC NEILLIE	8, 49, 89
MAC MINNIES	21, 49, 50	MAC NEIVE	67
MAC MONNIES	21, 49, 89	MAC NELLAN	8, 17, 89
MAC MONT	8	MAC NELLEN	89
MAC MORAN	37, 49, 50	MAC NELLIE	8, 49, 89
MAC MORELAND	36	MAC NENAMY	68
MAC MORINE	21, 28, 49	MAC NENE	68
MAC MORLAND	8, 37, 71, 89	MAC NESTER	WORCESTER, 1651, AM
MAC MORRIN	36	MAC NESTRIE	36
MAC MORRINE	36	MAC NESTRY	36
MAC MORRING	36	MAC NEW	87
MAC MUFFIN	8	MAC NIEL	5, 14, 45
MAC MUILLE	63	MAC NIELL	5, 67
MAC MULL	63	MAC NIFF	36, 37, 50
MAC MULLE	63	MAC NILLAGE	37, 50, 71
MAC MULLER	8	MAC NIMARA	37
MAC MULTY	68	MAC NO	36
MAC MUNAGALL	36	MAC NOAH	21, 89
MAC MUNAGLE	36	MAC NOBLE	41
MAC MURIN	37, 50	MAC NOE	21, 36, 49
MAC MURRIE	49, 67, 89	MAC NOLLY	36
MAC MYLER	8	MAC NOON	36
MAC MYNE	8	MAC NORMER	8
MAC NABBOW	5	MAC NORTON	87
MAC NABNEY	89	MAC NORWOOD	5
MAC NABO	5	MAC NOUIN	36
MAC NABOE	5	MAC NOWN	36
MAC NAE	21, 49	MAC NULTY	14, 20, 37
MAC NAIN	36	MAC NUNIGAL	37
MAC NALLY	36	MAC NUNN	36
MAC NAMEE	37, 50, 89	MAC OLANAICH	5
MAC NAUL	36	MAC OLASH	44
MAC NAULL	36	MAC OLVORIE	5
MAC NAVAGE	67	MAC OLVORY	5
MAC NAY	21, 49, 89	MAC OMBIE	1, 11, 58
MAC NEA	67	MAC OME	37, 50, 71
MAC NEATH	89	MAC ONISH	37, 50
MAC NEFF	36	MAC ONNICH	41
MAC NEIF	36	MAC ONNICK	41
MAC NEILEDGE	5, 50, 71	MAC ONOCHIE	28, 37, 56

SURNAME	DISTRICT	SURNAME	DISTRICT
MAC ONOGHOY	36	MAC PROUTIE	8
MAC ORMIC	37, 56, 88	MAC PROUTY	8
MAC ORMICK	8, 20, 23	MAC QUAIL	87
MAC ORT	16	MAC QUAILL	87
MAC OSCAR	37	MAC QUAILLS	87
MAC OSCARS	37	MAC QUALS	87
MAC OUAN	37, 67, 89	MAC QUATER	8, 37, 71
MAC OUTEREY	36	MAC QUEENY	75
MAC OUTERIE	36	MAC QUEIN	67
MAC OUTRIE	44	MAC QUEINE	67
MAC OUTRY	44	MAC QUERRIST	JACOBITE, 1747, AM
MAC OWIN	JACOBITE, 1716, AM	MAC QUESTIN	8
MAC PAGE	36	MAC QUETIE	36
MAC PAIK	87	MAC QUETTERS	68
MAC PAIKE	87	MAC QUETTIE	36
MAC PAKE	36	MAC QUETTY	36
MAC PARLANE	14, 88, 89	MAC QUETY	36
MAC PATE	36	MAC QUHA	50
MAC PAY	67	MAC QUHAEG	68
MAC PAYE	67	MAC QUIBAN	11, 47, 58
MAC PEACE	36	MAC QUIDDIE	36
MAC PEAK	23, 36, 71, 88	MAC QUIDDY	36
MAC PEAKE	36	MAC QUIDIE	36
MAC PECK	36	MAC QUIDY	36
MAC PEEK	36	MAC QUIG	36
MAC PERSON	1, 48, 89	MAC QUIGGAN	36, 37, 81, 89
MAC PHAILLATE	45	MAC QUILLAR	33
MAC PHARLANE	45, 63, 75	MAC QUILLER	33
MAC PHEARSON	14, 48, 67	MAC QUILLIE	42
MAC PHEAT	3	MAC QUILLIN	42
MAC PHEATORS	37, 50	MAC QUILLING	42
MAC PHEDRIES	8	MAC QUILLIS	16
MAC PHELIM	68	MAC QUIN	8, 37, 45
MAC PHELY	71	MAC QUIRK	83
MAC PHERON	36	MAC QUIRKE	83
MAC PHIDRAN	71	MAC QUISTEN	5, 8, 37
MAC PIKE	36	MAC QUISTIN	8
MAC PLOY	84	MAC QUISTON	5, 8, 14
MAC PRANGLE	31	MAC QUITTIE	36
MAC PROUD	8	MAC QUITTY	36
MAC PROUDE	8	MAC RABBET	36

SURNAME	DISTRICT	SURNAME	DISTRICT
MAC RABBIT	36	MAC ROSTY	37, 48, 67
MAC RABET	36	MAC RUDIN	23
MAC RABIT	36	MAC RUVIE	87
MAC RABIT	36	MAC RUVY	87
MAC RAFT	36	MAC SALLY	8
MAC RAILT	45	MAC SAUL	8
MAC RAVEN	36	MAC SAVERIE	8
MAC RAVENS	36	MAC SAVERY	8
MAC RAVIN	36	MAC SAY	87
MAC RAVINS	36	MAC SCORBIE	1
MAC READIE	8, 26, 36, 89	MAC SCORBY	1
MAC READY	3, 23, 36, 89	MAC SEPHNINE	37
MAC REAK	87	MAC SHAEFFREY	87
MAC REAKIE	87	MAC SHAND	1
MAC REAKY	87	MAC SHANE	DUNBAR, 1650, AM
MAC REDDIE	3, 28, 88	MAC SHAY	87
MAC REDIE	8, 26, 88	MAC SHEA	87
MAC REEKIE	87	MAC SHEAN	37, 81, 89
MAC REEKY	87	MAC SHEE	68, 87
MAC RICHARD	1	MAC SHEFFREY	37, 50
MAC RICHARDS	1	MAC SKELLIE	36
MAC RIDDIE	36	MAC SKELLY	36
MAC RIDDY	36	MAC SKIMMING	8, 37, 50
MAC RIDES	36	MAC SKULIN	67
MAC RIDGE	36	MAC SLARROW	67
MAC ROAN	36	MAC SLAY	67
MAC ROANE	36	MAC SLOY	44
MAC ROBIN	1, 89	MAC SOSEN	36
MAC ROCK	36	MAC SOUL	8
MAC RODDIE	36	MAC SOWL	8
MAC ROFT	36	MAC SPADDAN	8
MAC RON	21, 71	MAC SPADDEN	8
MAC RONALD	1, 8, 45	MAC SPADDER	16
MAC RONE	36	MAC SPEDDON	16
MAC ROSIE	67	MAC SPEDON	16
MAC ROSKIE	84	MAC SPEFFAN	16
MAC ROSKY	84	MAC SPERITT	5
MAC ROSS	86	MAC SPIRIT	5
MAC ROSSAN	84	MAC SPIRITT	5
MAC ROSSIN	84	MAC STADDEN	16
MAC ROSTIE	17, 28, 67	MAC STEVEN	75

SURNAME	DISTRICT	SURNAME	DISTRICT
MAC STOOT	36	MAC TURNER	36
MAC STOOTS	36	MAC UILLAN	15
MAC STOTT	1	MAC ULLOCH	75, 86, 89
MAC STOTTS	1	MAC URICH	ARGYLL'S REBELLION, 1685, AM
MAC STRAVICH	5		
MAC STRAVICK	5	MAC VAE	8, 49, 89
MAC STRAVOCH	5	MAC VAN	21, 49, 71
MAC STRAVOG	5	MAC VEETY	36
MAC STRAVOK	5	MAC VERIE	36
MAC STROUL	83	MAC VERRAN	ARGYLL'S REBELLION, 1685, AM
MAC STURGEON	36		
MAC SUET	36	MAC VETTIE	36
MAC SWEYER	36	MAC VETTY	36
MAC SWIGGAN	68	MAC VETY	36
MAC SWIGGANS	68	MAC VIETTIE	36
MAC TAILLIOR	67	MAC VIETTY	36
MAC TALDROCH	89	MAC VILLE	68
MAC TALIDEFF	1	MAC VINIE	49
MAC TAMNIE	5	MAC VITIE	21, 28, 36, 49
MAC TAMNY	5	MAC VITTIE	8, 20, 21, 36
MAC TARBBY	68	MAC VITTY	36
MAC TARBY	68	MAC VITY	36
MAC TARGET	28, 56, 89	MAC VUI	68
MAC TAY	67	MAC VUILLE	63
MAC TAYE	67	MAC VULL	63
MAC TERNAN	68, 87	MAC VUT	68
MAC TERNANA	37	MAC VYTIE	36
MAC TEY	67	MAC WALTERS	37, 50
MAC TEYE	67	MAC WARATY	5
MAC TIMMON	8	MAC WARNOCK	37
MAC TIMMOND	8	MAC WATERS	37, 50, 89
MAC TIMMONDS	8	MAC WATTY	20
MAC TIMMONS	8	MAC WERICH	74
MAC TOMANY	36	MAC WERICK	74
MAC TOMINAY	36	MAC WETHIE	36
MAC TOMNEY	36	MAC WETHY	36
MAC TULLDROCK	36	MAC WHAE	37, 49, 67
MAC TURCK	36	MAC WHANNEL	48, 67, 89
MAC TURK	8, 21, 36, 49	MAC WHARTER	8, 50
MAC TURNAN	36	MAC WHETIE	36
MAC TURNEN	36	MAC WHETTIE	36

SURNAME	DISTRICT	SURNAME	DISTRICT
MAC WHETTY	36	MACK ONE	WORCESTER, 1652, AM
MAC WHETY	36	MACK ONNE	WORCESTER, 1652, AM
MAC WHIDDIE	36	MACK SHANE	DUNBAR, 1650, AM
MAC WHIDDY	36	MACK TENTHA	WORCESTER, 1652, AM
MAC WHIE	21, 50	MACK TRETH	ROYALIST,
MAC WHINNY	20, 28, 56		WORCESTER, 1652, AM
MAC WHIR	21, 37, 49	MACK WATER	DUNBAR, 1650, AM
MAC WHITTIE	36	MACK WELL	WORCESTER, 1652, AM
MAC WIDDIE	36	MACLAINE	5
MAC WIDDY	36	MACXY	DUNBAR, 1650, AM
MAC WIGGIN	44	MAD ARDY	45
MAC WIGGINS	44	MAD DERMID	45
MAC WILL	16	MAD KENDRICK	48
MAC WILLEY	42	MAD KIDD	86
MAC WILLIAMS	37, 50, 71	MAD PHEDRAN	71
MAC WILLIS	16	MADDAN	23
MAC WITHEE	DUNBAR, 1650, AM	MADDEN	14, 23, 28, 37
MAC WITTIE	36	MADDER	21, 75, 87
MAC WITTY	36	MADDISON	20, 26, 48
MAC WOOLIE	36	MADDON	8, 20, 37
MAC WOOLY	36	MADER	87
MAC WORD	5	MADIGAN	50
MAC WORKMAN	33	MADOLAND	3, 5, 45, 75
MAC WORTH	5	MAGELBIE	36
MAC WURTHIE	5	MAGELBY	36
MAC WURTHY	5	MAGOON	DUNBAR, 1650, AM
MAC YARGAR	5	MAGRAGAN	83
MAC YARGER	5	MAGUIRE	33, 37, 49
MAC ZEEK	36	MAGUNNIGLE	37
MAC ZINC	36	MAHER	28, 47, 56
MAC ZINK	36	MAHON	8, 37, 50
MACK ALESTER	WORCESTER, 1652, AM	MAHONEY	37, 50, 71
MACK FASSY	DUNBAR, 1650, AM	MAHOOD	89
MACK HELLIN	WORCESTER, 1652, AM	MAICH	3, 23, 47
MACK HENE	WORCESTER, 1652, AM	MAIL	3, 37, 89
MACK HOME	WORCESTER, 1652, AM	MAILER	17, 48, 67, 84
MACK IAH	DUNBAR, 1650, AM	MAILEY	8, 26, 71
MACK ILUDE	WORCESTER, 1652, AM	MAILLER	23, 33, 48
MACK JAMES	(NFI) 1684, AM	MAIN	JACOBITE, 1747, AM
MACK LUDE	WORCESTER, 1652, AM	MAIR	50
MACK NEILE	WORCESTER, 1652, AM	MAISELS	87

SURNAME	DISTRICT	SURNAME	DISTRICT
MAISLETT	22	MAN	14, 26, 58, 67
MAISMYTHE	50	MANBY	58, 71
MAISON	87	MANCLARK	89
MAITHESON	45	MANCLERK	89
MAIZLAND	49	MANDERSON	26, 48, 75, 87
MAJOR	8, 24, 47, 56	MANDERSTON	28, 56
MAJORS	23	MANDEVILLE	67
MAKELLAR	26	MANFORD	37, 45, 71
MAKEN	67, 71, 89	MANLY	3, 23, 37
MAKER	75	MANNERS	20, 28, 33
MAKERSTOUN	75	MANNING	20, 37, 50
MAKERSTOWN	75	MANSELL	75
MALCHOLM	71	MANSFIELD	67
MALCOME	71, 89	MANTLE	3, 71
MALCOMSON	49, 67, 89	MANUEL	28, 56, 75, 89
MALE	46	MANWELL	26, 71, 89
MALES	46	MANZIE	1, 3, 33
MALHAM	28, 56	MAPPLEBECK	44
MALISE	1	MARCH	28, 56, 75, 87
MALL	75	MARCHAL	12, 23, 89
MALLACE	23	MARCHANT	3
MALLEN	20, 71, 75	MARCHER	87
MALLENIE	87	MARCOT	87
MALLENY	87	MAREN	87
MALLICE	17, 50, 89	MARGACH	85
MALLIE	1, 63, 67	MARGERIE	67
MALLIN	37, 50, 75	MARGERY	67
MALLIS	23	MARINER	21
MALLISH	23	MARJORYBANKS	21
MALLISON	23	MARK	67, 75, 77
MALLOCK	17, 23, 67	MARKER	1, 47, 71
MALLON	23, 28, 56	MARKIE	8, 28, 88
MALLONEY	JACOBITE, PRESTON, 1716, AM	MARKLE	22
		MARLEY	44
MALLONEY	5	MARLOW	8, 21, 58
MALLONIE	5	MARLY	71
MALLY	67, 71	MARMICK	44
MALONE	1, 23, 36, 89	MARNIE	3, 23, 47
MALOY	5, 12, 88	MARNOCK	1, 28, 37
MALTMAN	1, 12, 67, 89	MARQUIS	5, 20, 71
MALWEE	36	MARRAY	17, 86, 89

SURNAME	DISTRICT	SURNAME	DISTRICT
MARRIS	20, 23, 71	MAURICE	1, 28
MARSH	1, 8, 28, 75	MAVEN	1, 11, 12
MARSHBURN	87	MAVERS	1, 3
MARSTON	44	MAW	87
MARTEN	33, 71, 75	MAWE	87
MARTIAL	3	MAWER	3, 23, 67
MARTIE	33, 89	MAWHINEY	20
MARTINE	1, 26, 49	MAWSON	67
MARTINSON	28, 45, 71	MAXEY	DUNBAR, 1650, AM
MARTISON	JACOBITE, 1716, AM	MAXSY	DUNBAR, 1650, AM
MARVIN	44	MAXTONE	28, 56, 67
MARWOOD	37	MAXY	DUNBAR, 1650, AM
MARY	20, 21, 49	MAYBERRY	37, 50
MASSIE	1, 11	MAYER	33, 37, 50
MATCHES	67	MAYERS	84
MATCHET	37, 50	MAYKIRK	87
MATESON	1	MAYLEN	86
MATHEW	3, 23, 33	MAYLON	86
MATHEWS	1, 89	MAYOR	23
MATLACK	38	MEACHAN	37, 50
MATLOCK	38	MEAD	28, 56
MATTERS	3, 23, 50	MEAGLE	75
MATTHESON	1, 45, 71	MEAL	67, 69, 89
MATTHEW	1, 3, 23	MEALING	77
MATTHEWS	23, 49, 89	MEALL	3, 21, 23
MATTHEWSON	12, 15, 89	MEALMAKER	3, 23, 37
MATTHIE	14, 17, 71	MEALMAN	3
MATTHIES	14	MEAM	8
MATTHIESON	37, 67, 89	MEAME	8
MATTHISON	5, 67, 69	MEAN	12, 26, 67
MATTIESON	26, 86, 89	MEANY	DUNBAR, 1650, AM
MAUCHAN	83	MEARNS	1, 3, 68, 84
MAUCHLEN	12, 28, 68, 75	MEARS	84
MAUCHLINE	37, 50, 56, 68	MEARSE	1
MAUDE	37	MEARSON	89
MAUDSON	67	MEASON	10
MAUGHT	36	MECHAN	23, 37, 50
MAULDSLIE	83	MECHLANE	COVENANTER, 1684, AM
MAULDSLY	83	MEDDISON	3
MAULDSON	67	MEDLOCK	44
MAUND	36	MEECHAN	16

SURNAME	DISTRICT	SURNAME	DISTRICT
MEEHAN	16	MELON	20, 23, 89
MEEKEN	16	MELROSE	67, 75, 77
MEEKIE	1	MELROSS	26, 67, 75, 77
MEEKIN	16	MELROY	36
MEEKLE	67	MELTON	1, 47, 89
MEEME	8	MELVEEN	36
MEENY	DUNBAR, 1650, AM	MELVEL	15, 33, 48
MEFF	1	MELVIL	20, 23, 67
MEFFAN	3, 23, 47, 84	MELVILE	1, 33, 89
MEFFEN	1, 3, 23, 84	MELVILL	23, 33, 86
MEGGAT	8, 21, 31, 56	MEMES	3, 8
MEGGET	12, 31, 37, 56	MEMESS	47, 67
MEGGS	83	MEMMOTT	17
MEICKLE	8, 56, 88	MENAGH	37, 50, 71
MEIGGS	84	MENELAUS	28, 56, 71
MEIGHAN	16	MENMUIR	3, 26, 47
MEIGHEN	16	MENNON	12, 56
MEIGLE	67	MENNY	1, 3, 58
MEIKIE	33	MENTION	87
MEIKLAM	37, 71, 75	MENTIPLY	33, 71
MEIKLE	88	MERCHISTON	87
MEIKLEHAM	14, 37, 50	MERIAM	37
MEIKLEJON	33, 71, 89	MERK	37
MEIKLEM	36	MERKE	37
MEIL	3, 67, 71	MERLAY	75
MEILING	1	MERLIN	87
MEINE	75	MEROSE	75
MEIR	75	MERRETT	36
MEIRN	3	MERREYLEES	8
MEIRNS	3	MERRICK	36
MEKAN	36	MERRILEES	26, 28, 56
MELBURN	33	MERRIMAN	3, 67
MELCLERK	89	MERROW	DUNBAR, 1650, AM
MELDON	75	MERRY	5, 8, 14
MELLES	1, 20, 67	MERRYLEES	26, 71, 89
MELLEY	37, 50	MERRYMAN	16, 28, 56, 67
MELLIS	1, 11, 58	MERRYMOUTH	8
MELLISH	1	MERTHER	75
MELLOR	53	MERTON	1, 77
MELLOY	8, 20, 50	MESCHIN	83
MELLVILLE	1, 26, 37	MESS	1, 11

SURNAME	DISTRICT	SURNAME	DISTRICT
MESSENGER	36	MILLEGAN	8, 26, 49
MESSER	56, 67, 75, 89	MILLEN	14, 17, 23
MESTON	1, 47	MILLESON	3
METCALF	1, 26, 77	MILLHINCH	36
METCALFE	11, 28, 56	MILLHOLM	33
METHER	5, 56	MILLIDGE	15, 28, 56
METHUN	84	MILLIE	11, 33, 67
METHUNE	84	MILLIGAN	21, 49, 67, 89
METHVEN	3, 23, 33, 84	MILLIKEN	12
MEWERS	83	MILLONS	28, 56
MEYKIRK	87	MILLROY	21, 50, 88
MICHAN	20, 36, 37, 50	MILLSOP	8
MICHELL	49, 67, 89	MILMINE	89
MICHEY	JACOBITE, PRESTON, 1716, AM	MILNIE	1, 11, 47
		MILRAE	28, 36, 56
MICKELROY	36	MILRICK	8, 71
MICKLE	12, 75, 88	MILROY	8, 36, 49, 89
MICKLEROY	36	MILTON	11, 14, 58
MICKNAB	WORCESTER, 1652, AM	MILTOUN	(NFI) 1716, AM
MIDDLAR	1	MILVEN	1, 37, 89
MIDDLEMAS	26, 75, 88	MILWAIN	37, 49, 89
MIDDLEMASS	12, 26, 67, 75	MILWARD	67
MIDDLEMIS	12, 45, 75	MILWAY	36
MIDDLEMISS	12, 33, 67, 75	MILWIE	36
MIDDLEMIST	75	MIMY	DUNBAR, 1650, AM
MIDDLER	1	MINDRUM	75
MIDHOPE	75	MINER	83
MIEKLE	5, 33, 75	MINERS	83
MIEN	12, 56, 75	MINFORD	8
MIFFAN	28, 56	MINIMAN	33
MILBURN	33	MINNIE	1, 11
MILBURNE	33	MINNOCH	37, 49, 89
MILDRAIN	JACOBITE, PRESTON, 1716, AM	MINTIE	83
		MINTO	1, 17, 75
MILES	33, 75, 88, 89	MINTY	1, 11, 58, 83
MILFREDERICK	36	MINY	DUNBAR, 1650, AM
MILHENCH	36	MINZIES	49, 71, 75
MILLAM	67	MIRE	22
MILLANS	3, 23, 88	MIRK	37, 48, 71, 89
MILLARD	3	MIRLESS	36
MILLBURN	21, 75, 88	MIRRYLEES	26, 71

SURNAME	DISTRICT	SURNAME	DISTRICT
MIRTEL	35	MONFRIES	17, 26, 56
MIRTLE	35	MONILAWS	20, 21, 33
MITCHAEL	14, 33, 49	MONKTON	87
MITCHAL	8, 11, 58	MONORGAN	67
MITCHALE	33, 50	MONROW	WORCESTER, 1652, AM
MITCHEL	11, 33, 47	MONTAGUE	20, 23, 49
MITCHELHILL	56, 75, 77, 87	MONTFORD	1
MITCHESON	49	MONTGOMERIE	8, 37, 71
MITCHIE	1, 11, 20,	MONTHEATH	55
MITCHISON	26, 28, 45	MONTIER	87
MOAG	3	MONTIETH	71, 88, 89
MOCHAN	23	MONTITH	55
MOCHRIE	17, 28, 83, 88	MONTOUR	87
MOCHRY	83	MONWILLIAM	ROYALIST,
MODDIE	17, 45, 48		WORCESTER, 1652, AM
MOGGACH	85	MOODY	20, 67, 71
MOHAN	20, 23, 86	MOON	3, 23, 67
MOINE	68	MOONEY	20, 23, 71
MOINET	26, 28, 56	MOONLIGHT	1, 3, 47
MOIRA	44	MOOR	75, 77, 89
MOLES	49	MOOREHOUSE	37
MOLESON	1, 3	MOORMAN	83
MOLISON	1, 3, 47	MOORMEN	83
MOLL	75	MORAM	3, 20, 23
MOLLESON	71	MORAN	20, 23, 71
MOLLIGAN	21	MORCOT	22
MOLLINS	36	MORCOTT	22
MOLLISON	1, 3, 47	MORDISON	75
MOLLONS	49	MOREBATTLE	75
MOLLOSON	3, 23	MOREBURN	83
MOLONEY	28, 56, 71	MORECROFT	75
MOLVIE	33	MOREHEARD	83
MOLVY	33	MOREHOUSE	37
MOLYSON	28, 47, 56	MORELAND	3, 20, 49, 75
MONACHAN	8, 37, 88	MORESCROPE	87
MONAGHAN	37, 49, 89	MORETON	37, 50
MONCRIEFFE	28, 56, 67	MOREVILLE	87
MONDELL	87	MOREY	DUNBAR, 1650, AM
MONE	50, 67	MORHAM	27, 62, 56
MONELAWS	26, 28, 56	MORICE	1, 47
MONEY	20, 23, 71	MORIES	1, 63, 71

SURNAME	DISTRICT	SURNAME	DISTRICT
MORIN	8, 21, 23	MOXEY	28, 56
MORISON	45, 48, 75	MOYES	1, 3, 33, 48, 77
MORITZ	87	MOYHOUSE	33
MORLAND	36, 48, 49, 89	MOYLE	42
MORNIE	21, 33, 49	MOYNESS	18
MORNINGTON	83	MOYSES	1
MORNINGTONE	83	MUAT	23, 26, 89
MORPAT	83	MUCATOR	68
MORRAN	8, 21, 71	MUCH	89
MORRE	WORCESTER, 1652, AM	MUCHIE	89
MORRELL	75	MUCHY	89
MORRIE	5, 33, 47	MUCKARSIE	33
MORRILL	75	MUCKART	3, 37, 47
MORRIN	21, 45, 49	MUCKERSIE	67
MORRINE	21, 28, 49	MUCKLE	12, 56, 87, 89
MORRON	49, 71, 89	MUCKSTORE	JACOBITE, 1716, AM
MORROW	14, 49, 75, 89	MUDDIE	1, 23, 89
MORT	68	MUDGEON	36
MORTHERALL	83	MUDIE	3, 23, 67
MORTHLAND	8	MUDNELL	36
MORTY	3	MUGGAH	85
MORWICK	67	MUGGINS	3
MOSCRIP	12, 71, 75	MUIE	12
MOSES	1	MUIL	1, 17, 58, 63
MOSLEY	87	MUILL	63
MOSLIE	87	MUIRDEN	1, 58
MOSSGROVE	33	MUIRE	49, 50, 67
MOSSMAN	COVENANTER, 1678, AM	MUIRESON	67
MOTHERWELL	20, 71, 80, 89	MUIRHALL	83
MOTION	8, 14, 33	MUIRHED	50
MOUG	3	MUIRHOUSE	37
MOULD	5, 28, 33	MUIRIE	50
MOULTRAY	28, 33, 56	MUIRISON	1, 11
MOULTRIE	67, 87	MUIRS	33, 50, 67
MOULTRY	33, 87	MULDONICH	55
MOUNCEY	21, 49	MULDOON	3, 23, 50
MOUNCY	36, 49	MULHOLAND	23, 28, 37
MOUNSEY	75	MULHOLLAND	37, 49, 50
MOUNSIE	75	MULHOLM	37, 50
MOUNTREE	36	MULL	63
MOUTRAY	87	MULLAN	37, 50, 88

SURNAME	DISTRICT	SURNAME	DISTRICT
MULLAR	15, 67, 89	MURIE	33, 48, 67
MULLARKEY	36	MURIESON	1
MULLARKY	36	MURK	37
MULLAY	23, 28, 89	MURLAND	49
MULLENDER	21	MURPHAY	3, 23, 71
MULLENS	21, 28, 56	MURRISON	1, 11, 15
MULLER	28, 33, 37	MURRY	11, 26, 89
MULLEY	63	MURTIE	87
MULLHOLLAND	37, 50, 89	MURTY	87
MULLIKIN	67	MUSCHET	89
MULLIN	37, 50, 71	MUSGRAVE	28, 56
MULLINS	8, 28, 67	MUSKELL	36
MULLION	55	MUSKETT	17, 37, 50
MULLIONS	55	MUSSELBURGH	62
MULRYAN	36	MUSTARD	3, 67, 75
MULTHALLAN	36	MUTCH	1, 47, 89
MULTHALLEN	36	MUTCHIE	89
MULTRART	37	MUTCHY	89
MULTRAT	37	MUTER	23, 37, 50, 83
MULVEY	37, 50	MUTHAG	31
MUN	37	MUTRIE	14, 50, 71, 87
MUNCIE	15, 72, 75	MUTRY	87
MUNDALL	28, 49, 77	MUTTER	26, 56, 83, 88
MUNDEL	8, 21	MYALLS	75
MUNDELE	36	MYALS	75
MUNDELL	21 49, 67	MYERS	47, 49, 88
MUNDILL	36	MYLER	33, 36
MUNDIMUIRBURN	83	MYLES	3, 23, 33, 75
MUNDLE	21, 75	MYLLAR	36, 87
MUNGALL	50, 88, 89	MYLLES	3, 67, 75
MUNGLE	56, 71, 88	MYRE	22, 33
MUNGO	3, 21, 33	MYRTLE	28, 56
MUNOCH	50, 89	NAESMITH	3, 50, 56, 71
MUNSE	37, 50	NAILOR	37, 50
MUNSIE	8, 21, 37, 75	NAILSMITH	37
MUNSY	75	NAISMAITH	3
MURCAR	1, 45	NAISMITH	37, 50, 88
MURCHLAN	8	NAISMYTH	37, 88
MURCHLAND	8, 71	NAMARD	36
MURDIE	67, 75, 86	NASH	20, 33, 86
MURDISON	12, 37, 67	NASMITH	56, 71, 89

SURNAME	DISTRICT	SURNAME	DISTRICT
NASS	37	NEWBY	87
NAVIN	1, 20, 89	NEWCASTLE	87
NAY	8, 33, 49	NEWELL	28, 36, 37, 50
NAYLOR	3, 23, 37, 87	NEWER	36
NAYSMITH	3, 26, 28, 56	NEWHALL	36
NAYSMYTH	3	NEWLYN	36
NEAT	44	NEWMAN	1, 23, 47
NEATE	44	NEWTON	12, 23, 88
NEAVE	1, 3, 23	NEYSMITH	3
NEAVERIE	67	NIBLOCK	37, 50, 89
NEAVERY	67	NIBLOE	9, 21, 71, 89
NEDDRIE	3, 47	NICKLSON	26
NEE	36	NICOLE	3, 11, 23
NEEDHAM	8	NICOLL	3, 23, 48
NEILANCE	56	NIDDERIE	87
NEILANDS	28, 56	NIDDRAY	87
NEILANS	12, 26, 56	NIDDRIE	1, 3, 47
NEILLANDS	36	NIDDRY	87
NEILLANS	26	NIELD	36
NEILLON	68	NIELL	8, 26, 89
NEILSTON	8, 28, 71	NIELSTON	8
NEIR	68	NIGEL	37
NEISMITH	20, 71, 89	NIGELL	37
NELIS	28, 37, 71	NINIAN	8, 28, 36, 89
NELLINS	12	NISBIT	12, 23, 89
NELLIS	37, 50, 71	NITHERY	48
NESSAN	52	NITHSDALE	67
NESSEN	52	NITTERS	49
NETHERWOOD	8	NIVESON	20, 21
NETHERY	37, 50, 71	NIVIE	1, 58
NEVEN	8, 23, 75	NOE	36
NEVENS	28, 56, 89	NOLAN	5, 23, 71
NEVERY	JACOBITE, 1716, AM	NOLEN	44
NEVILL	37, 50	NOON	1
NEW	1, 3, 23	NOONE	1
NEWAL	21, 49, 67	NORAM	87
NEWALL	21, 23, 36, 49	NORCLIFF	87
NEWBERRY	8, 75, 77, 87	NORCLIFFE	87
NEWBIE	87	NORHAM	87
NEWBIGGING	12, 50, 67, 83	NORIS	23, 37, 50
NEWBURN	33	NORQUAY	67

SURNAME	DISTRICT	SURNAME	DISTRICT
NORREY	87	OGILVEY	3, 23, 67
NORREYS	87	OGLE	87
NORTH	87	OGLEBY	JACOBITE, PRESTON,
NORTHWOOD	5		1716, AM
NORTON	37, 50, 75	OGSTOUN	9
NORVIL	89	OIG	21
NORWOOD	5	O'LARGIE	5
NOTMAN	22, 28, 56, 67	OLD	67, 87
NUDDIE	33	OLDROYD	87
NUGENT	28, 49, 56	OLDS	67, 87
NUIR	36	OLLASON	89
NULTY	14	O'LONACH	5
NUNN	85	OLONIE	5
NUTALL	53	O'LONIE	5
NUTSHILL	37	OLSON	15, 37, 67
NUTTER	24	OMISTON	75
OAG	1, 15, 75	OMIT	56
OAK	1	OMOND	28, 67, 89
OAKE	1	ONEALE	WORCESTER, 1652, AM
OAKIE	1	ONKSTER	89
OAKLEY	3, 33, 37	OPRROCK	33
OASTLER	3, 47	ORAM	1, 3, 21, 67
OATE	55	ORCHARDSON	28, 47, 56
OATES	23, 28, 55, 71	ORCHESTON	1, 3
OATMAN	75	ORCHISTON	1
OATS	3, 23, 71	ORD	11, 12, 75
OATT	50, 71	ORDE	75
O'BRIAN	37	ORE	50, 63, 67
O'BRIEN	37	OREM	1
O'BROLOCHAN	5	ORGILL	36
OCCLESTON	87	ORKNEY	3
OCHERTON	1	ORMAN	12, 56, 75
OCKFORD	87	ORME	3, 23, 56
OCKMAN	89	ORMES	3, 23
ODIE	89	ORMINSTON	75
O'DONNELL	50	ORMISTON	26, 67, 75
OFFICER	3, 23, 47, 71	ORMISTONE	72, 75, 86
OGDAN	75	ORMOND	3, 28, 56, 86
OGDEN	75	ORMSTON	12, 45, 75
OGESTON	3	ORMSTONE	28, 56, 75
OGILL	87	O'ROURKE	5

SURNAME	DISTRICT	SURNAME	DISTRICT
ORPHANT	20, 26	PADGEN	87
ORRACK	28, 33, 88	PADKIN	48, 63, 77
ORTIN	44	PADYN	37
ORWELL	1	PADYNE	37
OSBORN	68	PAE	12, 28, 67
OSBORNE	8, 15, 67, 68	PAESTON	3
OSBOURGH	23	PAGAN	21, 49, 67
OSBOURN	37, 50, 89	PAGE	14, 33, 48
OSBOURNE	8, 37, 50	PAGET	37, 50
OSBURN	20, 21, 67, 75	PAIDLEY	48, 63, 77
OSBURNE	8, 71, 75, 89	PAIGE	33
OSLER	3, 23, 33, 71	PAIN	28, 49, 71, 78
OSTLER	33	PAINE	28, 49, 68, 89
OTTER	87	PAINTER	3, 23, 33, 48
OTTERBURN	75	PAIP	1
OTTO	21, 28, 56	PAIRMAN	28, 56, 67, 75
OUSTON	1	PAIRNIE	67
OUSTONE	1	PAKER	89
OUSTOUN	1	PALFREYMAN	62
OUTERSON	12, 26, 75	PALSON	DUNBAR, 1650, AM
OUTLAW	3	PANDRICH	3, 23
OUTRAM	44	PANMAN	28, 56
OUTRAY	44	PANTER	60
OUTRIE	44	PANTLER	68
OUTTERSTONE	12	PANTON	26, 48, 58, 87
OVANS	28, 37, 56	PAPE	44
OVENS	26, 22, 75, 77	PAPLE	17, 48, 63
OVENSTONE	33	PAPPIL	32
OVER	67	PAPPLE	21, 32, 49, 89
OWENS	12, 37, 48	PARDIE	DUNBAR, 1650, AM
OWER	3, 23, 67	PARDOVAN	87
OXLAY	85	PARIS	3, 8, 36, 63, 88
OXLEY	85	PARISS	8
PACCOCK	83	PARKER	8, 67, 71, 89
PACE	67, 75, 88	PARKHILL	8, 49, 71, 89
PACK	3, 15, 17	PARKIN	23, 37, 89
PACKER	37	PARKINS	3, 21, 49
PADDER	8	PARKINSON	44
PADDIE	37	PARKISON	21, 37, 50
PADDY	37	PARKS	8, 20, 89
PADGE	20, 33	PARLAN	37, 50, 89

SURNAME	DISTRICT	SURNAME	DISTRICT
PARLEY	3, 23, 75, 87	PEACE	67, 81, 89
PARNIE	37, 50, 67	PEACH	44
PARR	17, 26, 56	PEARTREE	21
PARROT	20, 37, 56	PEASE	75
PARROTT	37, 50	PEASTON	26, 56, 67, 87
PARRY	28, 56, 79	PEATIE	3, 28, 33, 56
PARSONS	DUNBAR, 1650, AM	PEATTY	3
PARTIE	89	PEATY	3
PARTINGTON	8	PEBBLES	3, 23, 58, 88
PARTRIDGE	63, 11, 37, 50	PECK	28, 44, 56, 71
PASELIE	68	PECKARD	88
PASELY	68	PEDDER	33
PASLEE	68	PEDDIN	8
PASLEW	68	PEDDY	33, 67
PASLEY	71, 75, 77, 78	PEDIE	26, 28, 56
PASLIE	68	PEDLEY	8, 89
PASLIG	68	PEEK	83
PASSELEWE	68	PEEL	20, 37, 49, 50
PASSELY	68	PEELE	36
PASTOR	75	PEERS	87
PATEN	8, 15, 17	PEFFERS	12, 22, 26, 28
PATIE	3, 33, 88	PEGGIE	1, 23, 33, 36
PATIENCE	28, 44, 75, 86	PEGLER	1
PATILLO	1, 23, 67	PELKAY	44
PATTENER	25	PELKEY	44
PATTENMAKER	37	PELLING	50
PATTERNER	25	PELLOW	8
PATTIESON	21, 71, 75	PENDAR	5, 71, 88
PATTILLO	1, 37, 67	PENDER	20, 37, 88, 89
PATTINER	25	PENDERGAST	87
PATTONSON	1	PENDERGRAST	87
PATTY	21, 37, 50	PENDIN	37
PAULET	87	PENDREICH	89
PAULETT	87	PENDRICH	26, 28, 56
PAULIN	3, 12, 49, 67	PENDRICK	23, 26, 89
PAULINE	3	PENDRIGH	12, 26, 56, 89
PAULING	49	PENEN	68
PAVEY	33	PENLAND	87
PAXTANG	87	PENMAN	17, 33, 75, 77
PAYNE	21, 28, 49	PENN	67, 71, 89
PAYTON	37, 50	PENNELL	8, 37, 50

SURNAME	DISTRICT	SURNAME	DISTRICT
PENNER	87	PETTINAIN	68
PENNERGAST	87	PETTINGER	34
PENNERGRAST	87	PETTIT	83
PENNET	18	PETTRIE	11, 33, 58
PENNEY	1, 20, 44, 67	PETTY	1, 83
PENNICUICK	28, 56	PETTYCREW	37, 50, 89
PENNIE	11, 23, 44, 48	PHELP	33
PENNMAN	12, 37, 50	PHIL	1
PENNY	1, 12, 17	PHILAN	83
PENON	68	PHILIPPS	56
PENRICE	20, 50, 89	PHILIPS	1, 23, 77
PENTON	36	PHILLANS	83
PENTONE	36	PHILLIP	1, 77, 89
PENYCOOK	3, 23, 56	PHILP	17, 33, 48
PEOCK	8, 20, 71	PHILPS	23, 33, 67
PEPDY	87	PHILSON	87
PEPPER	36	PHIMISTER	83
PEPPERMAN	68	PHIPPS	28, 56
PERCY	21, 67, 71, 89	PICARD	33
PERGITER	37	PICKANS	8
PERKIE	87	PICKARD	1, 3, 56
PERKIN	37, 50	PICKART	3, 56, 75
PERKINS	12, 28, 37, 56	PICKEN	8, 14, 71
PERKLE	87	PICKERING	20, 21, 50
PERKS	75	PICKETT	37, 50, 75
PERNESS	85	PICKIEMAN	37
PERRIE	3, 11, 47, 71	PICKING	1, 8
PERRIN	87	PICKMAN	33
PERRINE	87	PIERCY	3, 37, 50
PERRIS	37	PIERSON	87
PERRONS	53	PIGGIE	1, 33, 48
PERRY	3, 14, 37, 89	PIGGOT	87
PERT	3, 23, 49	PIGGOTT	87
PERTH	28, 56, 67	PIGOT	1, 3
PERVIS	87	PIKE	1, 2, 89
PETLEY	28, 56	PIKER	83
PETTECREW	26, 37, 50	PILCHEY	44
PETTERSON	71, 81, 89	PILCHIE	44
PETTICREW	8, 14, 89	PILCHY	44
PETTIE	1, 28, 56, 83	PILE	28, 37, 50
PETTIGREW	37, 50, 83, 88	PILINGER	44

SURNAME	DISTRICT	SURNAME	DISTRICT
PILLAN	28, 33, 56	PITTENDRICH	1, 47
PILLANS	56, 77, 83, 87	PITTENDRIGH	1, 47
PILLIANS	84	PITTIGREW	37
PILLING	33	PITTILLO	33
PILLINGER	44	PITTINGER	34
PILMER	3, 12, 17, 87	PLATT	5, 12, 28
PILMOR	3	PLATTER	3
PILMORE	87	PLAYER	3
PIMLOTT	45	PLENDERLEATH	12, 50, 75
PINDAR	37	PLENDERLEITH	12, 67, 75
PINDER	37	PLENDERLEITHLY	75
PINGLE	35	PLENDERLIETH	28, 50, 56
PINKIE	87	PLEWRIGHT	83
PINKSTON	20	PLEWS	28, 56
PINKY	87	PLOWMAN	15, 28, 56
PINMURRAY	JACOBITE, 1747, AM	PLOWRIGHT	83
PINNER	68	PLUMER	75
PINNEY	44	PLUMMER	28, 56, 75
PINNIE	44	PLUNKET	37, 50, 89
PIRIE	1, 4	PLUNKETT	37, 50
PIRNIE	3, 67, 88	POLAND	8, 71, 89
PIRNY	67	POLLAND	1, 88, 89
PIRRET	20	POLLEXFEN	28, 56, 67, 87
PIRRIE	1, 3, 11	POLLY	50
PITCAITHLEY	37, 50	POMFRET	83
PITCAITHLY	1, 33	POMHRET	85
PITCOCK	22	POMPHRAY	83
PITCOX	22	PONT	67
PITCULLO	33	PONTIE	44
PITH	87	PONTY	44
PITHIE	1, 3, 47	POOL	21, 28, 36, 37
PITHY	1	POOLE	3, 28, 36, 49
PITILLO	33, 67	POOLER	33, 89
PITKAITHLY	3, 23, 48	POOR	75
PITKEATHLIE	3	POORE	75
PITKEATHLY	3, 67	POPE	1, 44, 86
PITKETHLY	3, 23, 33, 84	PORTAR	38
PITT	8, 12, 17	PORTEOUS	21, 26, 67
PITTENDRAY	18	PORTEUS	20, 21, 89
PITTENDREIGH	18	POTT	21, 75, 86, 87
PITTENDREY	18	POTTAR	83

SURNAME	DISTRICT	SURNAME	DISTRICT
POTTERFIELD	68	PROCKTER	3
POTTIE	20, 33, 67	PROCKTOR	3
POTTS	49, 67, 75, 87	PROCTER	3
POUND	37	PROCTOR	3, 11, 58
POUNDS	37	PROFET	1
POURIE	3, 23, 67	PROFETT	1
POUSTIE	3, 33, 48, 87	PROFIT	3, 23, 47
POUSTY	87	PROPHET	1, 3, 15, 23
POW	26, 75, 77	PROSSER	1, 5, 50
POWELL	8, 17, 75	PROUD	17, 33, 48
POWER	DUNBAR, 1650, AM	PROUDFOOT	21, 67, 69, 87
POWRIE	3, 23, 67	PROUDIE	1
POWRY	3	PROUDY	1
PRAIN	3, 23, 67	PROVAN	20, 37, 67
PRATLEY	67	PROVAND	37
PRATTE	33, 37, 50	PROVEN	37, 77, 88, 89
PREACHER	26, 28, 67, 75	PROVEND	37
PREIR	68	PROVOST	3
PRENDERGAST	87	PRUDE	33, 56
PRENTICE	50, 67, 87, 88	PRYDE	15, 33, 56, 68
PRENTISS	87	PRYNN	68
PRESCOTT	75	PRYNNE	68
PRESFEN	75	PRYOR	23
PRESLIE	1	PTOLEMY	8, 71
PRESSLY	1	PUDSEY	68
PRESTWICK	8	PUISLEY	5
PRETSALL	35	PULLAR	3, 23, 67
PRETSEL	28, 56, 67	PULLER	20, 23, 67
PRETSELL	28, 56, 67, 35	PULSON	1, 11, 21
PRETT	33, 50	PUNDLER	67
PREY	37, 50	PUNN	22
PRICE	11, 44, 49, 89	PUNTON	12, 23, 26, 87
PRIDE	26, 33, 68, 88	PURDIE	49, 67, 75, 88
PRIEST	33, 58, 75, 77, 89	PURDOM	37, 75
PRIESTLY	33, 75	PURDON	37, 71, 75
PRIESTON	67	PURDY	75
PRIOR	23	PURGAVIE	3, 23
PRIORS	23	PURROCK	23
PRISK	15	PURSE	48, 63, 77
PRITCHARD	1, 8, 56	PURSELL	5, 8, 56
PROBERT	1, 8, 37	PURVIES	87

SURNAME	DISTRICT	SURNAME	DISTRICT
PYKEER	83	RAMSON	1
PYLE	20, 21, 75, 83	RANDAL	3, 23, 89
PYTES	5	RANDLE	33
QUARLES	87	RANISON	1
QUAYS	15	RANKEN	14, 17, 77
QUENTIN	75	RANKING	20, 71, 77
QUERNE	22	RANKS	11, 28, 56
QUIGLEY	37, 71, 89	RANNOLDSON	2
QUIGLY	8, 21, 71	RANSON	1, 28, 56
QUINCY	33	RAPHAEL	21, 37, 50
QUINNEY	26	RAPIER	1, 47
QUINON	75	RARITY	8, 28, 56, 88
QUINTON	5, 33, 71	RASH	JACOBITE, 1716, AM
QUIRE	36	RASIDE	8, 36, 71, 89
RABAN	44	RATHBURN	37
RABBAN	44	RATTOR	28, 56, 75, 89
RACH	37	RAVENSHEN	15
RADCLIFF	20	RAVEY	36
RAEPER	1	RAVIE	8, 14, 20
RAESIDE	8, 36, 71, 89	RAWLIN	49, 67
RAFF	1, 37, 45, 58	RAWLINE	21
RAFFAN	1, 11, 23, 85	RAWLING	67
RAFFARTY	21, 37, 50	RAWLINGS	67
RAFFEL	49	RAWLINSON	88
RAFFERTY	21, 49, 71	RAWSON	28, 37, 45, 87
RAFFLES	67	RAWTON	36
RAGG	1, 17, 44	RAYNES	36
RAIGMORE	44	READDIE	33, 67
RAILSON	8	READHEAD	1, 77
RAILSTON	20	READMAN	26, 75
RAIN	21, 49, 89	REAPER	1, 11
RAINIE	1, 11, 58	REARIE	8
RAINNIE	1, 11, 58	REAVIE	8, 38, 50
RAINY	1, 11	REDAR	33
RALEIGH	28, 49, 56	REDARE	33
RALLENDRA	WORCESTER, 1652, AM	REDDEN	12, 75
RALPH	45, 58, 63	REDDENS	75
RALTON	21, 89	REDDICK	21, 49, 50
RAMAGE	17, 26, 48, 87	REDDIE	3, 33, 48, 88
RAMSDEN	75	REDDIN	75
RAMSDON	75	REDDINS	75

SURNAME	DISTRICT	SURNAME	DISTRICT
REDDY	3	RENTOUL	28, 48, 50, 56
REDER	33	RENWICK	67, 75, 77
REDFERN	37, 44, 49, 50	REPER	1
REDIE	3	REPPER	1
REDPATH	12, 26, 75, 87	RESIDE	8, 71, 89
REDSHAW	87	RESTON	22, 36
REDY	3	RETSON	36
REECE	36	RETTIE	1, 10, 11
REEDER	67, 88	RETTY	10
REEDIE	28, 33, 56	REUEL	33
REEKIE	3, 23, 33, 67	REVICH	37
REEKY	3	REVIK	37
REEL	33	REW	3, 47, 67
REES	36	REWCASTLE	75
REETH	44	REWELL	33
REEVE	83	REYBURN	8
REEVES	83	REYLEY	15
REEVIE	37, 50	REYLIE	86
REGAN	37, 49, 50	REYLY	86
REIDIE	33	REYNARD	50
REIDPATH	75	REYNOLD	52
REIFF	33	REYNOLDSON	2
REIKIE	28, 33, 56	RHENIUS	67
REILLY	1, 20, 50	RHIND	1, 24, 58
REKIE	3, 33	RHINE	11, 20, 37
RELLIE	87	RHYND	33, 37, 58
RELLY	87	RIANSFORD	49
REMSON	37	RICCALTON	87
RENDAL	67, 81, 89	RICCALTOUN	87
RENDELE	5	RICCOCK	11
RENDELL	5, 33	RICE	37, 71, 89
RENELE	33	RICH	1, 67, 89
RENFREW	20, 50, 78, 71	RICHARD	3, 8, 20
RENFREY	68	RICHARDS	21, 28, 37, 83
RENFRO	68	RICHARSON	21, 37, 56
RENISON	37	RICHIE	23, 26, 88
RENNEY	3, 58, 67	RICHIESON	62
RENNIESTON	75	RICHMAN	1
RENNISON	21, 37, 50	RICHMOND	8, 37, 71, 80
RENNOCH	67	RICHMONT	8
RENTA	37	RICHORDS	83

SURNAME	DISTRICT	SURNAME	DISTRICT
RICKARD	3, 28, 47	RIX	67
RICKART	1	ROACH	5
RICKERT	1	ROADVILLE	75
RICKETS	21, 37, 75	ROAN	21, 49, 89
RICKETTS	28, 37, 56	ROARK	3, 37, 50
RICKLESTON	87	ROAST	1
RICKSON	44	ROBBS	28, 56
RIDDAL	1	ROBERSON	3, 67, 89
RIDDELE	75	ROBERT	3, 47, 89
RIDDET	8	ROBERTON	48, 50, 75
RIDDLER	3, 23, 47	ROBIE	1, 3, 47
RIDER	8, 23, 75	ROBIESON	1, 21, 49
RIDGARD	68	ROBIN	48, 67, 89
RIDGE	22	ROCHE	87
RIDLER	1	ROCHEAD	20, 28, 67
RIDPATH	12, 26, 75, 77	ROCK	87
RIED	8, 20, 67	ROCKALL	67
RIELLY	8, 28, 56	RODAN	8, 21, 67
RIGBY	1, 56	RODDAM	12
RILEY	20, 28, 37	RODDAN	21, 37, 49, 67
RIMMER	84	RODDEN	21, 28, 36, 75
RIMMON	44	RODDICK	3, 15, 21
RIMORE	75	RODDIE	17, 36, 37, 89
RIND	28, 33, 56	RODDY	36
RINNIE	1, 47	RODEAK	36
RINTOUL	17, 33, 48, 55	RODGER	3, 33, 71, 77
RINTOULL	28, 33, 88	RODGERS	3, 37, 50, 89
RIPON	1	RODGIE	1, 28, 67, 75
RIPPON	1	RODGY	1
RIRE	71	RODICK	23, 88, 89
RIRIE	1, 15	RODIE	8, 37, 89
RISTON	75	RODMAN	8, 20, 71
RITCH	15, 67, 89	ROE	8, 37, 48
RITCHARDS	28, 56	ROGAN	21, 49, 58
RITCHISON	12, 81, 89	ROGER	3, 23, 33, 47, 75
RITCHLEY	8	ROGERS	3, 28, 49, 56, 75
RITCHLIE	8	ROGERSON	1, 20, 21, 49
RITCHLY	8	ROGGIE	44
RITSON	36	ROGGY	44
RITTLER	1	ROGIE	3, 44, 47, 67
RIVER	75	ROGY	44

SURNAME	DISTRICT	SURNAME	DISTRICT
ROLFE	36	ROTHNEY	1, 11
ROLL	1	ROTHNIE	1
ROLLAN	1	ROTHNY	1
ROLLAND	1, 3, 17, 33	ROUGH	1, 3, 67, 83
ROLLIE	1, 33, 71	ROUGHEAD	28, 56, 89
ROLLIN	3, 33	ROUGHHEAD	87
ROLLINGS	75	ROUGVIE	28, 56, 71
ROLLINS	75	ROURK	47, 71, 89
ROLLISON	5, 28, 56	ROURKE	20, 37, 50
ROLSON	3	ROUSAY	67
ROMANE	75	ROUTLEDGE	75
ROMANES	28, 56, 77	ROW	83
ROMANIS	28, 33, 75	ROWAN	8, 14, 37
ROMANS	1, 56, 75	ROWAND	20, 37, 71
ROME	21, 36, 49, 75	ROWAT	8, 20, 37, 50
RONEY	36	ROWATT	8, 21, 37, 89
RONNAN	52	ROWE	1, 12, 21, 83
RONNEY	87	ROWEN	3, 23, 49
ROOK	86	ROWIE	28, 58, 89
ROOKE	86	ROWLAND	1, 67, 75, 89
ROOKES	86	ROWLEY	8, 28, 56
ROOKS	86	ROWSAY	67
ROOM	5	ROXBORO	75
ROOME	5	ROXBURGH	8, 21, 33, 75
ROON	37	ROYAN	20, 45, 58
ROONE	37	ROYDEN	68
ROONEY	20, 23, 37	ROYE	7
ROOPTON	8	RUAN	75
ROOT	36	RUCASTLE	75
ROOTE	36	RUCKBIE	75
ROOTEY	36	RUCKBY	75
ROPER	1, 20, 28, 67	RUD	14, 50, 89
ROPPER	1	RUDDERFORD	75
RORRIE	3, 89	RUDDIMAN	1, 11
RORRISON	8, 21, 49	RUDDOCH	1, 11, 58
ROSEWELL	87	RUDDOCK	36
ROSLYN	87	RUDGE	44
ROSSITER	87	RUDIMAN	1
ROSWELL	87	RUDOLF	37, 50
ROSYTH	33	RUDOLPH	37, 50
ROTHESAY	74	RUE	1, 26, 89

SURNAME	DISTRICT	SURNAME	DISTRICT
RUFF	83	SADLIER	75
RUFFUS	87	SAFELY	28, 36, 37, 56
RUGG	15, 67	SAFFLEY	21, 56
RULSTON	5	SAFLEY	37, 56, 71
RULSTONE	5	SAGAN	36
RUMBLES	11	SAGE	33
RUMBOLD	1, 85	SAIDLER	37, 50, 75
RUMGAY	3, 23, 33	SAITH	28, 33, 56
RUNCEMAN	12, 26, 28	SALER	75
RUNCHIE	1, 8, 21	SALKRIG	87
RUNCIEMAN	75	SALKRIGE	87
RUNCIMAN	12, 26, 75, 77	SALLEY	37, 89, 89
RUNEY	1, 3	SALLY	36
RUPTON	8	SALMON	14, 20, 67, 71
RUSHWORTH	28, 56	SALMOND	3, 33, 67, 88
RUSKY	67	SALTER	1, 33, 62, 67
RUSLAND	67, 89	SALTON	26, 56, 67
RUSSLAND	28, 67, 89	SALVUNA	36
RUST	1, 47	SAMPLE	8, 12, 75
RUSTE	1	SAMPSON	8, 24, 47, 83
RUTHERGLEN	83	SAMSON	3, 8, 23, 83
RUTLEDGE	1, 49, 58, 75	SAMUELS	28, 56
RUTTER	26, 67, 75	SAND	33
RUXTON	1, 3, 23	SANDALL	75
RYAN	36, 37, 58, 89	SANDEMAN	3, 23, 67
RYANS	8, 37, 50	SANDIESON	11, 58, 67
RYDALE	35	SANDIFORD	20
RYDER	12, 23, 28, 56	SANDMAN	67
RYE	1	SANDOCK	87
RYMER	33, 56, 87	SANER	87
RYMORE	87	SANG	1, 28
RYMOUR	87	SANGSTER	1, 88
RYRIE	15, 28, 56	SANKIE	75
RYSLAND	8	SANKY	75
RYSTON	75	SANSON	87
RYSTOUN	75	SANSTER	1
SABISON	67	SANUNDERSON	12
SACHIE	55	SAUCER	89
SACKETT	68	SAUCHIE	55
SADDLER	21, 47, 75	SAUCIERE	89
SADLER	3, 23, 67, 75	SAUL	21, 49, 89

SURNAME	DISTRICT	SURNAME	DISTRICT
SAUNDERS	3, 23, 48	SCOTTLAWN	3
SAUNDERSON	23, 77	SCOUGAL	3, 12, 28, 56, 62, 87
SAVAGE	8, 49, 89	SCOUGALL	56, 62, 67, 77, 87
SAVIDGE	87	SCOULAR	8, 36, 37, 48, 88
SAVILLE	87	SCOULER	36, 37, 50, 67
SAWER	8, 37, 89	SCOULLER	8, 37, 50
SAWERS	8, 26, 89	SCRAMBLE	36
SAWYER	21, 28, 56	SCRIMGEOR	3, 28, 67
SAWYERS	37, 49, 88	SCRIMGOUR	3, 23, 67
SAYERS	28, 49, 87, 88	SCRIMM	67
SCADLOCK	68	SCROGGIE	1, 23, 47
SCAIFE	87	SCROGGINS	23
SCALES	17, 28, 36, 49	SCROGGS	75
SCALLIE	5	SCROGGY	23, 37, 50
SCALLY	5	SCROGIE	1, 11, 47
SCAMBLE	36	SCRULTON	1
SCANIAN	37, 50, 71	SCULLY	15
SCANLANDERS	58, 71, 89	SCUNY	33
SCARLET	48, 71, 75	SDEUARD	67
SCARLETT	26, 67, 71	SEALER	75
SCATTERTY	1, 58	SEARGENT	71
SCEALES	28, 56	SEARLE	23
SCHAW	8, 28, 56	SEARLES	23
SCHEILL	87	SEARSON	50
SCHOFIELD	37, 50, 58	SEATHE	33
SCHOOLBRAID	28, 67, 69	SEBASTIAN	28, 37, 50
SCHOOLBREAD	33	SEELER	75
SCHOOLBRED	33	SEIRVIN	37
SCHOOLER	1, 12, 71	SEIRVINE	37
SCHULTZE	28, 37, 56	SEIVWRIGHT	3, 11, 89
SCLATER	1, 11, 67, 89	SELBIE	1, 47, 87
SCLATTER	28, 67, 89	SELBOURNE	85
SCOBBIE	17, 48, 67	SELBY	1, 47, 87
SCOFFIELD	37, 50	SELCRAIG	36
SCOFIELD	1, 37, 50	SELKIRK	17, 21, 26, 75
SCOLLICK	8, 50	SELLAR	1, 11, 58
SCONE	67	SELLARS	1, 14, 37, 50
SCOON	21, 67, 75, 77	SELLER	1
SCORGIE	1, 47	SELLERS	1, 14, 37, 77
SCORGY	1	SELVIN	37
SCOTLAND	3, 17, 33, 48	SENIOR	3, 23, 33, 75

SURNAME	DISTRICT	SURNAME	DISTRICT
SERLE	67	SHEA	53
SERLES	67	SHEAL	75
SERVANT	1, 49	SHEARAR	1
SERVICE	8, 12, 20, 55	SHEARIN	75, 89
SESSOR	22	SHEARLAW	12
SETTER	28, 56, 67	SHEARSMITH	1
SEWALL	75	SHEARWOOD	5, 23, 56
SEWAR	1	SHEDAN	8
SEWART	11, 63, 75	SHEDDAN	5, 8, 28
SEWELL	75	SHEDDEN	8, 67, 71
SEWER	1	SHEDDON	8, 26, 71
SEXTON	26, 71, 88	SHEDEN	8
SEYBOLD	33	SHEDON	8
SEYMORE	22	SHEEN	50, 75
SEYMOUR	8, 71, 88	SHEERIN	49
SHADDEN	37	SHEERLAW	12
SHADDON	37	SHEILD	3, 23, 37
SHADE	28, 37, 56, 87	SHEILL	17, 26, 75
SHAFTO	87	SHEILS	37, 50, 88
SHAFTOE	87	SHEIPP	68
SHAID	28, 56	SHELDON	26, 50, 67
SHAIRP	28, 75, 88	SHELDRICK	5
SHAKELOCK	3	SHELLIE	85
SHAKLOCK	3	SHELLY	85
SHALCROSS	15	SHELMERDINE	36
SHALE	87	SHELTON	28, 47, 56
SHAND	1, 11, 58	SHENNAN	21, 49, 89
SHANK	11, 36, 77, 87, 89	SHEPHARD	11, 17, 75, 88
SHANKIE	28, 56, 67	SHEPHERD	1, 47, 75
SHANKLEY	26, 50, 71	SHEPPARD	1, 28, 67
SHANKLY	28, 56, 75	SHERAR	1, 67
SHANKS	36, 58, 87, 88, 89	SHERAT	1, 3, 47
SHANKY	67	SHERATT	71
SHANLEY	37, 50	SHERE	1
SHANNAN	20, 21, 89	SHERET	1, 3, 47
SHARER	63, 81, 89	SHERFFS	1
SHARKEY	8, 71, 88	SHERIDAN	17, 28, 37
SHARKIE	67, 71, 89	SHERIF	3, 28, 58
SHARMAN	1	SHERIFF	1, 12, 26, 88
SHARON	44	SHERIFFS	1, 47
SHARROCH	JACOBITE, 1716, AM	SHERIFFSON	22

SURNAME	DISTRICT	SURNAME	DISTRICT
SHERIFS	1	SHIRLAW	8, 37, 50, 83
SHERIFSON	22	SHIRLEY	12, 37, 71, 80
SHERLAW	12, 20, 26, 83	SHIRRA	37, 50, 89
SHERMAN	47, 49, 89	SHIRRAN	1, 11
SHERON	44	SHIRRAS	1
SHERRAT	1, 47, 71	SHIRREF	1
SHERRATT	1	SHIRREFF	1, 26, 67
SHERRIF	1, 3, 28, 56	SHIRREFFS	1
SHERRIFF	12, 26, 67	SHIRREFS	1
SHERRIFS	1, 47	SHIRRER	1
SHERRIT	3	SHIRRES	1, 11
SHERWIN	1	SHISH	88
SHERWOOD	17, 23, 67	SHIVAS	1
SHETTLETON	37, 50	SHIVERS	28, 37, 50
SHEWAN	1, 47, 89	SHIVES	1
SHEWEN	1	SHONER	33
SHEY	5	SHONEY	33
SHIEFFE	87	SHONGER	JACOBITE, PRESTON, 1715, AM
SHIEL	75, 77		
SHIELD	1, 3, 23, 87	SHONIE	33
SHIELDS	8, 37, 87, 88	SHONRE	33
SHIELL	12, 67, 75	SHOOLBRED	33, 48
SHIELLS	26, 28, 56, 75	SHORE	58, 75, 88
SHIELS	12, 26, 75, 88	SHORROCK	36
SHIERLAW	83	SHORT	12, 33, 75, 89
SHILESTON	67	SHORTE	89
SHILLING	26, 28, 37	SHORTER	8
SHILLINGLAW	12, 28, 56, 87	SHORTHOUSE	21, 33, 48, 50
SHINNE	WORCESTER, 1652, AM	SHORTREDE	28, 56
SHINNIE	1, 71	SHORTREED	67, 75, 77
SHINNON	8, 28, 56	SHORTREID	12, 56, 75
SHIPLAW	87	SHORTRIDGE	21, 49, 67, 71
SHIPLEY	20, 56	SHORTT	21, 28, 86
SHIRAR	8	SHOTTEN	28, 56
SHIREFF	28, 56, 75	SHOWAN	1
SHIREFFS	1, 47	SHOWEN	1
SHIRER	1	SHUNGER	3
SHIRESS	3, 33	SHURRON	44
SHIRET	3	SHUTTARD	JACOBITE, PRESTON, 1716, AM
SHIRKIE	71		
SHIRKY	8, 20, 71	SHUTTIE	3, 8

SURNAME	DISTRICT	SURNAME	DISTRICT
SHYNE	28, 56	SKELLY	8, 71, 89
SIBBALL	33	SKELTON	1, 21, 48
SIBBARD	75	SKEOCH	8, 21, 71
SIBBERD	75	SKERREL	36
SIBBULD	33	SKETHWAY	37, 67, 69
SIDY	3, 23, 71	SKEY	83
SIERS	26, 71	SKID	DUNBAR, 1650, AM
SIEVEWRIGHT	1, 11, 47	SKILLING	8, 71, 89
SIEVWRIGHT	11, 47, 89	SKIMMING	8, 36, 49, 89
SILLAR	7	SKINNERS	23, 33, 88
SILLARS	5, 7, 8, 14	SKIPPER	1
SILLER	7	SKIRKEY	37, 50
SILLERS	7	SKIVENTON	49
SILLIVEN	36	SKIVINGTON	37, 50
SILVER	1, 3, 47	SLACK	75
SILVESTER	80	SLADE	28, 56, 71
SILVIE	3, 28, 89	SLAKER	1, 11
SIMES	11, 20	SLATE	26, 28, 56
SIMKIN	89	SLATER	1, 11, 67, 77
SIMM	14, 58, 71	SLATTER	1, 67, 75, 89
SIMMIE	28, 56, 67	SLATTERY	28, 56
SIMMINGTON	83	SLAVEN	37, 50, 71
SIMONSON	89	SLAY	1
SINCLAR	5, 67, 89	SLAYROCK	1
SINGER	1, 23	SLAYWRIGHT	1
SINGERS	3, 33, 69	SLEAGER	1
SINGLETON	37, 49, 67, 87	SLEIGH	1, 26, 28, 88
SINNOT	36	SLEIGHT	28, 56, 67
SIVAS	1	SLESSER	1
SIVES	1, 12, 26, 75	SLESSON	1
SIVESS	26, 28, 56	SLESSOR	1, 7
SIVEWRIGHT	1, 11, 63	SLESSUR	1
SIWES	87	SLIDDERS	3, 17, 23
SKAIR	1, 3	SLIDER	87
SKEAD	28, 50, 56	SLIDERS	17
SKEDD	62	SLIGH	12, 26, 88
SKEGGIE	37	SLIGHT	12, 26, 28, 87
SKEGGY	37	SLIGO	26, 67, 89
SKEGIE	37	SLIMAN	8, 50, 88
SKEGY	37	SLIMMAN	87
SKELDON	8, 12, 26, 36, 45	SLIMMON	21, 28, 67, 69

SURNAME	DISTRICT	SURNAME	DISTRICT
SLIMON	21, 23, 28, 56	SNADON	17, 56
SLLINKSKELL	12	SNAPE	83
SLOAN	68	SNEATH	28, 56
SLOANE	36, 49, 67, 89	SNEDDAN	87
SLOSS	1, 8, 37	SNEDDEN	20, 37, 50, 87
SLOVEWRIGHT	67	SNEDDON	17, 37, 50, 87
SLOWAN	8, 14, 67, 89	SNELL	1, 5, 20, 37
SLUDER	36	SNEY	1
SLYMON	23	SNIDDON	37, 50
SMAILL	26, 75, 88	SNODGRASS	20, 49, 71
SMALES	28, 56	SNOWDEN	87
SMALLEY	37	SNOWDON	87
SMALLWOOD	68	SNOWIE	1, 47
SMEALL	28, 56, 88	SOFFLEY	67
SMEATON	17, 26, 48	SOFTLAW	36
SMELLIE	5, 67, 83, 88	SOFTLY	36
SMELLY	83	SOKAN	67
SMETON	17, 33, 89	SOMERVILL	17, 20, 67
SMETTAM	12	SOMMERS	26, 50, 67
SMETTON	3, 23, 67	SOMMERVAIL	12, 28, 56
SMIBERT	87	SOMMERVELL	26, 50
SMILBERT	28, 56, 67	SOMMERVILE	14, 17, 67
SMILLEY	68	SOMNER	12, 26, 87, 89
SMILLIE	8, 50, 78, 71	SONGSTER	1
SMISON	WORCESTER, 1651, AM	SOOPER	1
SMITHSON	15, 37, 67	SOOT	3, 23, 67
SMITTON	17, 48, 67	SORBIE	21, 36, 48, 49
SMOLLET	3, 11, 23	SORBY	36
SMYLES	28, 56	SORELY	1, 17
SMYLIE	5	SORLAY	89
SMYLLIE	1, 3, 8	SORREL	3
SMYLY	5	SORRIE	1, 5, 8, 58
SMYTH	12, 23, 50	SORRY	8
SMYTHE	5, 33, 67	SOSSER	89
SMYTON	67	SOTHELAND	WORCESTER, 1652, AM
SMYTTAN	28, 56	SOUDIE	44
SMYTTON	67	SOUDY	44
SNADDAN	50, 88, 89	SOUNES	26
SNADDEN	17, 87, 88, 89	SOUNESS	26, 28, 56
SNADDON	17, 88, 89	SOUPER	1, 47
SNADEN	17, 37, 50	SOURLEY	56, 71

SURNAME	DISTRICT	SURNAME	DISTRICT
SOUTHHOUSE	87	SPOTTISWOODE	28, 33, 67
SOUTHLAND	86	SPOTTS	22
SOUTHWICK	36	SPOUSE	12
SOWDAN	75	SPOWART	1, 33, 88
SOWDEN	75	SPRAT	12, 75, 89
SOWERBY	15	SPRATT	12, 75, 89
SOWNESS	87	SPREUL	5, 71, 89
SPADDEN	1	SPRING	1, 47, 89
SPADEN	1, 28, 56	SPRINGER	1
SPAIN	87	SPROAT	21, 36, 49, 89
SPALDIE	1, 3, 88	SPROT	12, 26, 89
SPANG	37	SPROTT	23, 36, 75, 89
SPANKIE	3, 23, 86	SPROULE	8, 71, 89
SPANKY	23	SPROULL	37, 50, 71
SPARK	1, 12, 47	SPROUNT	3
SPARKES	1	SPROUT	36
SPARKS	1, 12, 71, 88	SPRUCE	67
SPEARS	12, 26, 56	SPRUNT	3, 23, 33, 67
SPEDDING	35	SPY	20, 67
SPEDEN	33	SQUARE	33, 63, 67, 89
SPEDIN	33	STABLE	3
SPEED	3, 33, 37, 67	STABLES	3
SPEEDEN	33	STACK	8, 28, 56
SPEEDIE	33, 48, 88	STAFFIN	36
SPEEDIN	33, 67	STAFFORD	34
SPEEDY	23, 33, 67	STAGE	28, 47, 56
SPEERS	20, 71, 89	STAGG	67
SPEID	1, 3, 23	STAIG	28, 33, 67, 69
SPEIR	8, 37, 71	STAIN	20, 83
SPENCER	5, 47, 67	STAINES	28, 56
SPERLING	68	STAINTON	75, 89
SPERLINS	68	STALKERS	3, 26
SPICER	28, 56, 89	STANFIELD	87
SPIDEN	26, 28, 75	STANFORD	37
SPIE	89	STANHOPE	49, 67, 87, 89
SPIER	8, 71, 75	STANHOUSE	28, 33, 48
SPILEMAN	1	STANLEY	26, 28, 87, 89
SPIRLING	68	STANNERS	26, 88, 89
SPOORS	37	STANTON	5, 37, 50
SPOTISWOOD	87	STARGEON	36
SPOTT	22	STARRS	37, 50

SURNAME	DISTRICT	SURNAME	DISTRICT
STATER	12	STOBBS	JACOBITE, 1716, AM
STAUNTON	37, 50	STOBBY	87
STAVERT	67, 75, 77, 87	STOBHILL	30
STEADMAN	28, 48, 56	STOBIE	12, 33, 48, 87
STEAL	37, 50, 71	STOBO	37, 50, 67
STED	1, 89	STOBY	87
STEDMAN	3, 20, 48, 75	STOCKAN	67
STEED	8, 28, 56	STOCKS	26, 33, 48
STEEDMAN	3, 28, 33, 48	STODART	12, 56, 67
STEELE	26, 36, 45, 87, 88	STODDARD	28, 36, 56, 89
STEELL	20, 71, 88	STODDART	12, 36, 67, 77
STEEPLES	28, 56	STODDERT	36
STEILL	87	STOKAR	1
STELL	1, 17, 21	STOKER	1
STENTON	20, 67, 75	STONE	28, 67, 75, 89
STERET	8	STONESTRADE	1
STERETT	8	STONIER	44
STERN	37	STONSTRADE	1
STERNS	37	STONYER	44
STEVENSTON	8, 26, 77	STOOPS	26, 37, 50
STEVENTON	28, 56, 67	STORER	48
STEVIN	15, 23, 89	STORKS	86
STICKLER	3, 23, 67	STORM	11, 58, 63
STIELL	37, 50, 75	STORMOND	3, 23, 67
STIEN	17, 67, 88	STORMONTH	3, 23, 28
STIL	62	STORRAR	28, 33, 18, 48
STILL	1, 11	STORRER	33, 48, 67
STILLIE	28, 56, 62, 89	STORREY	8, 28, 88
STILLY	62	STORRY	21, 75, 88
STINTON	3, 28, 56	STORY	12, 21, 75
STIREY	8	STOTHART	21, 28, 75
STIRRIT	71, 89	STOTT	1, 47, 89
STIRTON	3, 33, 67, 88	STOTTERD	37
STITCHEL	75	STOTTS	1
STITT	21, 31, 49, 89	STOUT	5, 67, 89
STIVEN	3, 23, 47	STOVE	20, 67, 89
STIVENS	3, 23, 28	STOW	87
STOAT	17, 23, 75	STOWART	33
STOB	67	STOWE	87
STOBBIE	23, 33, 67, 87	STOWELL	28, 56
STOBBO	12, 37, 50	STOWIE	75

SURNAME	DISTRICT	SURNAME	DISTRICT
STPEHENS	88	SUMMERHILL	87
STRAHORN	8	SUMMERVILL	20, 49, 67
STRAITH	1, 47	SUMPTER	67
STRAITTON	1, 3, 23	SUNTER	28, 33, 67, 71
STRALOCH	1	SUPER	1
STRANACK	1	SUSTER	68
STRATHAIRN	37	SUTAR	3
STRATHARN	37, 50, 75, 84	SUTHER	15, 28, 56
STRATHDEE	11, 47, 58	SUTTON	12, 20, 28, 36
STRATHEARN	23, 67, 84, 88	SWAINSON	89
STRATHENDRY	33	SWANAY	67
STRATHERN	37, 50, 88	SWANEY	20, 37, 67
STRATHIAIRN	50	SWANKIE	36
STRATHIE	28, 36, 55, 56, 67, 88	SWANNY	37, 50, 67
STRATHORN	3, 8	SWANSEY	2
STRATHY	28, 36, 55, 56, 67, 88	SWANSTON	12, 28, 67, 77
STRATTOUN	87	SWANSTONE	26, 28, 75, 88
STRAUCHON	12	SWANTON	26, 30, 67, 75
STRAWBRIDGE	8, 89	SWAYNE	28, 33, 56
STRAWHORN	8	SWEENIE	37, 71, 89
STREET	26, 28, 89	SWEENY	20, 37, 71
STRICKLANDS	22, 68	SWEET	20, 37, 75
STRICKLE	37	SWELLIE	37
STRICKLER	37	SWELLY	37
STROAK	JACOBITE, 1716, AM	SWIFT	20, 37, 50, 87
STROCK	JACOBITE, 1716, AM	SWINDLEY	87
STROTHER	3, 23, 33, 87	SWINFORD	37
STROYAN	36	SWINGER	JACOBITE, 1716, AM
STRUTH	28, 33, 48	SWINHOE	8
STRUTHERS	37, 50, 67, 87	SWINLEY	33, 67
STUBBS	1, 21, 23	SWINTOUN	COVENANTER, 1685, AM
STUPART	17, 28, 89	SWIRLES	3
STUPERT	8	SWITT	87
STURDY	3, 23	SWITTE	87
STURRICK	3	SWORD	23, 67, 77
STURROCK	3, 23, 47	SWORDS	67
STYLES	1, 67	SYARE	37
SUDDEN	12, 33, 75	SYDE	33
SULLIVAN	20, 23, 37	SYDESERF	26, 37, 50
SUMERVILLE	33, 37, 50	SYDIE	3, 23, 67
SUMMER	28, 33, 50	SYDSERFF	37, 50

SURNAME	DISTRICT	SURNAME	DISTRICT
SYLVIE	3	TAP	45
SYLVY	3	TAPPER	56
SYMES	37, 50	TARBAT	3, 23, 88
SYMINTON	26, 49, 75	TARBET	3, 71, 75
SYMM	1, 20, 50	TARLETON	33, 37, 50
SYMONDS	1, 28, 56	TARLTON	50
TABER	28, 56	TARR	44
TABOR	28, 56	TARRAS	1, 20, 44
TABURNER	87	TARRY	87
TACKER	88	TARVET	28, 33, 56
TACKET	67	TARVETT	33
TAGG	20, 37, 50	TARVIT	33
TAGGAT	49	TARVITT	33
TAGUE	8, 37, 50	TASKER	3, 23, 67, 87
TAILOR	15, 67, 75	TASSIE	37, 50, 67
TAILZEFIER	36	TASSY	37
TAINCH	22, 50, 67	TASTARD	1
TAITT	12, 75	TATENEL	1
TAKET	75, 77	TATENELL	1
TALBERT	1, 3, 37	TATTERSALL	37, 50
TALBOT	3, 56, 75	TAVENDALE	43, 47
TALFER	83	TAVERNER	87
TALLACH	33, 45, 86	TAVERNOUR	87
TALLEY	87	TAYBURN	67
TALLIE	87	TAYLEO	87
TAME	87	TAYMAN	67
TANCRED	87	TEACHER	83
TANISH	67, 89	TEALING	3
TANKARD	87	TEALLING	3
TANKERD	87	TEASDALE	21, 50, 67
TANNACH	20	TEASE	71
TANNER	3, 23, 87, 89	TEES	37
TANNIELL	WORCESTER, 1651, AM	TELFAIR	21, 71
TANNIS	67	TELFAR	21, 49, 71
TANNISH	67	TELLER	22
TANNOCH	8, 14, 71	TELLIE	36
TANNOUR	87	TEMAN	1
TANNYHILL	8	TEMPEST	33
TANPARD	37	TEMPLE	48, 62, 75, 77
TANPARDE	37	TENDEMAN	67
TANT	28, 56	TENDER	3

SURNAME	DISTRICT	SURNAME	DISTRICT
TENDMAN	67	THOMISON	3, 67
TENLER	22	THOMLING	36
TENLOR	WORCESTER, 1651, AM	THORBURN	36, 67, 75, 77, 89
TENNOCK	8, 37, 50	THORN	12, 20, 37
TERM	20	THORNBURN	8, 21, 50
TERRACE	28, 33, 88	THORNE	3, 37, 50, 86
TERRAL	1, 71	THORNESON	36
TERRAS	23, 33, 44, 56	THORNHILL	67
TERRES	1, 3, 33	THORNS	49
TERREY	60	THORNSON	36
TERRIES	1, 50, 88	THORNTON	3, 23, 88
TERRIS	33, 44, 48, 88	THORPE	1, 17, 28, 56
TERRY	7, 33, 58, 60	THORS	1
TERSE	1	THORSKLE	67
TERSIE	1	THOW	1, 3, 47
TERSY	1	THOWE	1
TERVET	50	THOWES	1
TERVIT	33, 50, 56, 68	THOWLESS	3
TERVITT	68	THREFALL	5
TESTARD	1, 47	THRESHIE	8, 21
TESTER	1, 47	THRIEPLAND	28, 56, 87
TESTOR	1	THRIFT	3, 23, 67, 87
TEVENDALE	3, 28, 47	THRIPLAND	50, 67
TEVENDEL	3	THRISLIE	33
TEVIODALE	28, 47, 56	THRIST	83
TEVIOTDALE	75	THROW	87
THACKER	1	THURBURN	11, 21, 58
THAINE	89	THYNE	28, 37, 56, 83
THATCHER	1	THYNNE	83
THAW	1, 28, 33, 47	TIBBERMORE	63
THAWE	1	TIEFNEY	37
THAWES	1	TIERNEY	28, 50
THEMAN	1	TILER	22
THEYNE	37, 50	TILLERY	1
THIEM	87	TILLEY	67
THIERRY	89	TILLIE	58, 75, 77, 87
THIN	87	TILLIS	28, 56
THIRD	1, 23, 89	TILLOCH	17, 20, 37
THIRLSTANE	87	TILLOTSON	44
THIRLSTON	87	TILLY	12, 37, 87, 88
THOIRS	67	TIMMINS	37, 50

SURNAME	DISTRICT	SURNAME	DISTRICT
TIMMONS	87	TOLLAR	37
TIMON	49	TOLLARE	37
TIMPANY	8, 71	TOLLER	37
TIMPSON	44	TOLLETH	28, 56, 67
TINCH	67	TOLLINS	37, 50
TINCTOR	67	TOLMIE	45, 63, 75
TINDAL	3, 23, 47	TOLMY	3, 58, 75
TINDALL	3, 12, 26, 87	TOMISON	67
TINDELL	3, 37, 50	TOMNEY	37, 50, 71
TINEDALL	87	TOMNY	37, 50
TINKER	67	TOMPSON	12, 37, 50
TINLAW	12	TONAR	8, 28, 56
TINLIN	12, 28, 75	TONER	63
TINLINE	67, 75, 77	TONGE	44
TINLING	21, 75, 77	TONGUE	44
TINMAN	68	TONNY	28, 56, 71
TINN	3, 33, 37	TOOK	3, 87
TINNEY	37, 71, 89	TOOKE	3, 87
TINNING	21, 49, 67	TOOLAN	35
TINNISWOOD	75	TOOLE	20, 28, 37
TINNOCK	83	TOOT	36
TINSMAN	8	TOOTE	36
TINTO	6, 9, 20, 21	TOP	1
TIPPING	71	TOPLESH	44
TIRNEY	37, 50	TOPLESS	44
TIVENDALE	33	TOPLIE	37
TIVERTON	33	TOPLIS	44
TIVOTDALE	28, 56	TOPLISH	44
TOAL	44	TOPLISS	44
TOBBERMORE	63	TOPLY	37
TOCHER	1, 11, 12	TORBET	12, 23, 89
TOCK	87	TORBURN	8, 36, 56, 89
TODDIE	30	TORBURNE	36
TODDY	30	TORK	(NFI) 1684, AM
TODRICK	87	TORLEY	37, 50, 89
TODSHALL	87	TORPHICHEN	28, 56
TODSHELL	87	TORRANCE	8, 87, 89
TOFTS	12, 26, 28, 75	TORRENCE	23, 28, 56, 87
TOISH	DUNBAR, 1650, AM	TORY	1, 26, 58
TOLAN	20, 37, 50	TOSSACK	28, 33, 56
TOLBERT	1	TOUCH	1, 3, 67

SURNAME	DISTRICT	SURNAME	DISTRICT
TOUCHE	1	TRIPNEY	28, 88, 89
TOUGHY	1	TRODDAN	8, 28, 49
TOUNG	44	TRODDEN	8, 49, 50
TOURIE	67	TRODDIE	67
TOURLEDGE	36	TRODDY	67
TOURS	67, 71, 89	TRODIE	67
TOVTDALE	3	TRODY	67
TOWER	1, 87	TROLLOPE	67
TOWERS	1, 67, 71, 87, 89	TRUEMAN	75
TOWN	87	TRUMAN	75
TOWNEND	44	TRUSTIE	36
TOWNLEY	50, 75	TRUSTY	36
TOWNLY	20, 33	TUCKEY	56
TOWNS	3, 23, 47, 87	TUDHOPE	50, 75, 77
TOWNSEND	28, 37, 50	TUKE	3, 23, 87
TOWNSLEY	5, 88, 89	TULIBO	1
TOWRIE	12, 33, 67	TULLAS	33
TOY	23, 37, 50	TULLIDEFF	1
TOYLE	67	TULLIDEPH	1
TRABOUN	87	TULLISH	33
TRACEY	36, 37, 50, 71	TULLOH	33, 58, 75
TRACY	3, 23, 36, 49	TULLY	75, 86, 88
TRAQUAIR	20, 67, 69	TUNNA	28, 56, 75
TRAQUIR	87	TUNNAH	12, 26, 75
TRAVIS	37, 49, 50	TUNNICK	36
TRAYLE	1	TUNNIE	12, 26
TREASONER	45	TUNNOCH	8, 50, 89
TREASURER	33, 58, 75	TUNNOCK	75
TREBUN	87	TUNNY	28, 37, 56
TREBUNE	87	TUNSTALL	42
TREMBLIE	3	TURBETT	83
TREMBLY	3	TURBITT	83
TRENANT	87	TURBYNE	26, 37, 50
TRENCH	87	TUREFF	1, 47
TREVELYN	87	TURFACE	67
TREVOR	67	TURFUS	37, 67
TREW	67	TURIFF	1, 47, 71
TREWMAN	75	TURING	1
TREWNOT	36	TURK	37
TRICKET	15	TURKE	37
TRICKITT	15	TURNET	75

SURNAME	DISTRICT	SURNAME	DISTRICT
TURPIE	3, 23, 28, 33	URCHILE	67
TURPIN	3	URCHILL	67
TURPNEY	COVENANTER, 1685, AM	URQUAHART	75, 89
		URQUART	3, 23, 33
TURSE	1	URWELL	44
TUSKER	44	USHAR	3
TUTHILL	85	USHER	3, 12, 75, 77
TWADDEL	21, 37, 50	USHERWOOD	37, 50
TWADDELL	87	USSHAR	3
TWAIN	19	USSHER	3
TWAT	67, 89	UTTERSON	12, 87, 88
TWEDDAL	28, 56, 89	VAIR	67, 75, 77
TWEDDEL	26, 71	VALANCE	8, 26, 71
TWEDDLE	21, 50, 89	VALANTINE	3, 23, 47
TWEDLE	37, 50	VALE	36
TWEED	87	VALENCE	12, 56, 77
TWEEDMAN	12	VALENTE	52
TWEEEDALE	87	VALENTINE	1, 3, 47
TWENTYMAN	21	VALENTNE	3
TWIGG	8, 21, 71	VALENTYN	3
TWINAME	49	VALINTINE	1, 3, 23
TWINDALE	68	VALLANCE	3, 8, 12, 26, 33
TWORT	5	VALLENCE	1, 12, 26
TWYNHOLM	21, 49	VALLENTINE	3
TYLER	22	VALLENTYN	3
TYNINGHAM	22	VALLENTYNE	3
TYNINGHAME	22	VALLEY	37, 67, 89
TYREE	67	VAN HESTON	28
TYRIE	48, 67, 69	VANCE	8, 36, 37, 71
TYSON	5, 12, 49, 75	VANDAL	71
TYTLER	1, 3, 87	VANN	1, 28, 33, 47
UDALE	21	VANNAN	3, 17, 20, 88
UDSTON	83	VANNET	3, 17, 33
UDSTONE	83	VANNIN	3
ULBRAND	68	VANS	28, 36, 56, 89
UNDERHILL	12, 71	VARY	21, 37, 50
UNES	36	VASSIE	50, 56
UNTHANK	12	VASSIR	8
UNWIN	75	VAUGHAN	23, 67, 71
UNWINE	75	VAUGHN	1
UPTON	28, 56, 89	VAUS	62

SURNAME	DISTRICT	SURNAME	DISTRICT
VAUSS	62	WADDEL	33, 87
VEITCH	56, 67, 77, 87	WADDELE	33, 87
VELZIAN	67	WADDELL	12, 20, 33, 50, 77, 87, 88
VENNAL	1	WADDIE	28, 56, 71, 75
VENTER	88	WADDIES	75
VENTURES	33	WADDLE	12, 23, 50
VERLE	75	WADDY	75
VERNEL	53	WADDYS	75
VERNER	87	WADE	1, 71, 89
VERNON	28, 36, 49, 89	WADIE	3, 56
VERT	26, 28, 56, 87	WAFERER	83
VERTH	26, 87	WAGAN	50
VERTIE	1, 3, 8, 26, 33	WAGGREL	1
VERTTIE	1, 3	WAGHORN	83
VERTTY	1, 3	WAGSTAFF	8, 71, 77
VERTY	1, 3	WAINEY	28, 56
VESEY	56, 83	WAITT	3, 8, 82
VESIE	83	WAKE	36
VESSEY	83	WAKERIE	3
VESSIE	1, 14, 56, 83	WAKERY	3
VESSY	56	WALACE	15, 17, 49
VETCH	75, 87	WALCH	17, 33, 50, 87
VICARS	17, 67, 75, 89	WALD	67
VICKERMAN	36	WALDEN	8, 12, 37
VICKERS	21, 28, 56, 75	WALDEVE	75
VIETCH	28, 56, 75	WALDGRAVE	1
VILE	36	WALDIE	12, 75, 77
VILKIE	33	WALDRON	75
VILLIE	42	WALDY	75
VINCENT	21, 50, 71	WALES	1, 8, 14, 36
VINT	36	WALFORD	75
VIRTUE	12, 17, 26	WALLER	33, 71, 89
VITCH	87	WALLET	8, 67, 69, 81
VIVERS	21	WALLINGFORD	75
VOCAT	1	WALLRAND	75
VOGAN	75	WALLS	17, 33, 67
VOLLAR	1	WALMSLEY	20, 28, 88
VOLLER	1	WALSH	23, 71, 75, 77
VOLUME	3	WALSHE	1
VOY	12, 67, 69	WALSTON	87
WABSTER	1, 26, 88	WALTHEW	75

SURNAME	DISTRICT	SURNAME	DISTRICT
WALTON	8, 20, 33, 53	WARRENDAR	33
WANCE	80	WARRICH	1
WAND	8, 14, 37	WARRICK	1
WANDERSON	11, 33, 48, 89	WARRINGTON	33, 37, 71
WANLESS	3, 12, 23, 87	WARROCK	1
WANLISS	87	WARSE	15
WANLISSH	87	WARTLIE	8
WANN	1, 23, 33, 87	WARTLY	8
WANNAN	23, 33, 67	WARWICK	21, 36, 49, 89
WANNCE	80	WASFORD	16
WANNS	80	WASTIE	33
WANS	80	WASTWOOD	33
WANTON	33, 48, 67	WASTY	33
WARD	37, 50, 67, 75	WATER	15, 49, 89
WARDE	28, 56, 75	WATERSON	3, 28, 48, 89
WARDEIN	33	WATERSTON	3, 33, 48, 71
WARDEN	3, 23, 33, 71	WATERSTONE	12, 48, 88
WARDHAWK	36	WATERSTOUN	3
WARDHOOK	36	WATERSTOUNE	3
WARDIE	26, 77, 89	WATERTON	3, 28, 56
WARDIN	33	WATHERSRONE	56
WARDLE	1	WATHERSTON	5, 12, 77
WARDOP	1	WATHERSTONE	12
WARDRAP	1	WATKINS	28, 37, 67
WARDROPE	1, 50, 88, 89	WATLING	28, 45, 56
WARDROPER	33	WATMAN	3, 23
WARDS	15, 67, 89	WATMORE	26, 37, 88
WARHAUGH	75	WATRET	21, 36
WARIN	83	WATTER	1, 56, 58
WARINER	37	WATTERSON	20, 26, 89
WARK	14, 75, 87, 88	WATTERSTON	26, 56, 88
WARKE	87	WATTERSTONE	45
WARLEY	8	WATTLE	1, 47
WARNER	37	WATTLING	26, 33
WARNES	83	WAUGHTON	87
WARNOCH	37	WAY	12, 33, 88
WARNOCK	37, 50, 71	WAYNESS	56, 75, 77
WARRACK	1	WEAD	3, 7, 23
WARRAND	44	WEAR	26, 75, 77
WARRANDAR	33	WEATHERHEAD	12, 28, 75, 87
WARRANDER	33	WEATHERLY	22

SURNAME	DISTRICT	SURNAME	DISTRICT
WEATHERSON	12, 75	WETHERSTON	12, 75, 77
WEATHERSPOON	3, 33	WEYMESS	33
WEATHERSTON	12, 67, 75, 87	WEYMS	3, 23, 33
WEATHERSTONE	12, 67, 75, 87	WHAIR	86
WEBBER	3, 23, 28, 56, 75	WHAMOND	3, 23, 28
WEBESTER	1, 3, 23, 88	WHANNEL	3, 8, 89
WEDD	37, 50	WHARRY	COVENANTER, 1689, AM
WEDDEL	12, 49, 88	WHEAR	15
WEDDELL	28, 67, 75, 87	WHEELAN	3, 23, 37, 75
WEDDEN	68	WHEELANS	75
WEDDERLIE	87	WHEELEN	50
WEDDERLY	87	WHEELER	5, 14, 33
WEDDERSPOON	20, 33, 67	WHEELWRIGHT	75
WEDDLE	87	WHEIR	15
WEDDOW	3, 83	WHELAN	75
WEDOW	3, 83	WHELANS	75
WEEDEN	75	WHENT	1
WEEDON	75	WHGHAM	75
WEIGHTON	3, 23, 67	WHIER	15
WEILD	21	WHIGAM	21, 26, 49, 87
WELCH	12, 33, 75, 87	WHIGHAM	21, 26, 49, 87
WELHAM	36	WHIGHAME	75
WELLAND	3	WHIGHT	36
WELLANDS	3	WHILELAW	22
WELLHAM	36	WHILLAN	75
WELSH	49, 67, 75, 77	WHILLANS	21, 75
WESTALL	1	WHILLES	28, 56, 67
WESTBURY	87	WHILLIS	12, 67, 88
WESTELL	1	WHIN	36
WESTEN	36	WHINTON	8, 37, 50
WESTFALL	1	WHIPPO	83
WESTGARTH	87	WHIRK	49, 89
WESTIE	33	WHITBY	87
WESTLAND	1, 42, 17	WHITEBURN	87
WESTLANDS	42	WHITEBURNE	87
WESTMAN	44	WHITECROSS	1, 23, 26
WESTNESS	67	WHITEHALL	37, 50, 71
WESTON	28, 36, 88, 89	WHITEHEAD	12, 17, 26, 22
WETHERBURN	1	WHITEHILL	37, 48, 67, 71
WETHERHEAD	33	WHITEHOPE	75
WETHERSPOON	17, 63, 88	WHITELOCK	37, 50, 75, 87

SURNAME	DISTRICT	SURNAME	DISTRICT
WHITELY	71	WICKUM	87
WHITESIDE	8, 71, 80, 89	WIDDENS	37
WHITESMITH	87	WIDDOW	83
WHITEWELL	36	WIDOW	83
WHITEWRIGHT	49	WIELD	21
WHITFIELD	21, 50, 67	WIER	5, 67, 89
WHITING	87	WIGGINS	37
WHITLEY	45, 75	WIGHT	12, 26, 75, 87
WHITLIE	12	WIGHTEN	28, 56
WHITSIDE	37, 50	WIGHTMAN	12, 21, 26, 87
WHITSLADE	75	WIGHTON	3, 23, 67
WHITSOM	12, 75	WIGMORE	87
WHITSOME	12	WILD	1
WHITSON	26, 67, 75, 77	WILDE	1
WHITSUNDAY	28, 56	WILDGOOSE	1, 11
WHITTAKER	1, 50, 71	WILDRIDGE	15, 33, 56, 87
WHITTEN	3, 26, 37, 48, 75	WILDSMITH	87
WHITTET	23, 44, 48, 67	WILGUS	1
WHITTIN	37, 75	WILIE	67, 71, 87, 89
WHITTING	87	WILKEN	1, 21
WHITTINGHAM	62	WILKES	12, 28, 56
WHITTINGHAME	62	WILKIESON	3, 12, 67
WHITTINGTON	28, 56	WILKIN	1, 20, 21
WHITTIT	28, 56, 67	WILKINS	3, 23, 89
WHITTLE	89	WILKISON	37, 49, 71
WHITTLE	33	WILKS	8, 28, 56
WHITTOCK	67	WILLANS	37, 50, 75
WHITTON	3, 23, 75	WILLARD	33
WHITTUN	75	WILLET	8, 16, 44, 67
WHITWORTH	75	WILLETS	16, 44
WHOLECOT	75	WILLIAM	1, 11, 75
WHOLECUT	75	WILLIANS	26, 56, 75
WHYNTIE	11	WILLIS	12, 28, 36, 88
WHYTEHEAD	37, 48, 50	WILLISON	36, 67, 77, 88
WHYTICK	87	WILLISSON	36
WHYTOCK	3, 23, 67, 87	WILLOCK	1, 8, 37, 47
WHYTT	28, 56	WILLOCKS	1, 3, 8, 23, 47
WICKEM	87	WILLOUGHBY	36
WICKENDEN	36	WILLOXS	1
WICKETSHAW	87	WILLSHOT	42, 87
WICKHAM	87	WILTON	67, 75

SURNAME	DISTRICT	SURNAME	DISTRICT
WINCHELL	87	WITTET	33, 44, 48, 67
WIND	3, 23, 37	WITTON	75
WINDER	37, 50	WODDROP	31
WINDRAM	3, 12	WODROW	5, 37, 50, 71
WINDRICK	67	WOGAN	36
WINFIELD	89	WOLF	23
WINGATE	17, 20, 37, 89	WOLFE	8, 23, 37, 50
WINGFIELD	1, 37, 50	WOLFSON	44
WINGO	1	WOLLER	75
WINING	8, 20	WOLLOX	37
WINK	1, 58	WONDER	3
WINKIE	37, 75, 89	WONDERS	3
WINKS	3, 23, 45	WOODALL	36
WINLAW	12, 67, 77	WOODCOCK	23, 33, 37, 49
WINN	37, 50, 56	WOODELL	36
WINSETT	44	WOODERSPOON	67
WINSLEY	1, 21, 88	WOODFIELD	67
WINT	87	WOODFORD	75
WINTER	3, 12, 23, 87	WOODGATE	56
WINTERS	12, 56, 71, 87	WOODHALL	3, 23, 87
WINTHROP	75	WOODHAW	87
WINTHROPE	75	WOODHEAD	28, 50, 56, 83
WINTIE	1	WOODHOUSE	21, 37, 50
WINTOUN	62	WOODLE	75
WINTOUR	87	WOODMAN	1, 11, 33
WINTOURS	87	WOODMAS	37, 50
WINTROPE	75	WOODMASS	21, 37, 50
WINTRUP	75	WOODRINGTON	75
WINTY	1	WOODROW	37, 49, 71, 75
WINWICK	89	WOODRUFF	37
WISE	1, 14, 23, 47	WOODSIDE	8
WISELY	1, 11	WOODSON	87
WISEMAN	3, 11, 50, 58	WOODWARD	44
WISHERT	23, 67, 89	WOODWELL	50
WISTON	83	WOOLDRIDGE	87
WITCOMB	11	WOOLDRIGE	87
WITHER	5, 36, 37, 89	WOOLFE	JACOBITE, 1716, AM
WITHERINGTON	JACOBITE, 1716, AM	WORDIE	89
WITHERS	36	WORDY	89
WITHERSPOON	17, 20, 88	WORK	1, 33, 67, 89
WITTER	44	WORLAND	71

SURNAME	DISTRICT
WORSFIELD	44
WORTHINGTON	20, 33
WOTHERPOON	COVENANTER, 1685, AM
YORK	37, 50, 75
YORKE	26, 67,
YORKSON	12, 26, 75
YORKSTEN	87
YORKSTIN	87
YORKSTON	26, 28, 87, 89
YORKSTONE	26, 28, 56
YORLK	12
YORSTAN	87
YORSTEN	87
YORSTIN	87
YORSTON	26, 67, 89
YORSTOUN	87
YORTON	87
YOU	12
YOUL	48, 67
YOULL	8, 11, 23
YOUNGCLAUSE	89
YOUNGHUSBAND	44
YOUNGSON	1, 54, 47
YOUNIE	11, 58, 67
YOURSTOUN	87
YUILE	37, 50, 67
YUILL	37, 50, 89
YULLO	83
YUNNIE	1
YURSTOUN	36
ZIMMERMAN	67
ZUILLE	20

APPENDICES

APPENDICES

APPENDIX A
Scottish District Naming Convention Pre-1890 to Present Day

Pre 1890 County/District	(1) County/Districts 1890 to 1975	(2) Regions 1975 to 1996	(2) Districts in Regions 1975 TO 1996	Council Areas as of 2022
Aberdeenshire	Aberdeenshire		Aberdeen, City of	Aberdeenshire
Argyll	Angus		Banff and Buchan	Aberdeen
Ayrshire	Argyll	GRAMPIAN	Gordon	Angus
Banffshire	(Forfarshire until 1928)		Kincardine and Deeside	Argyll and Bute
Berwickshire	Ayrshire		Moray	Ayrshire, East
Bute	Banffshire		Badenoch and Strathspey	Ayrshire, North
Caithness	Berwickshire		Caithness	Ayrshire, South
Clackmannanshire	Bute		Inverness	Clackmannanshire
Cromartyshire	Caithness	HIGHLAND	Lochaber	Dumfries and Galloway
Dumbartonshire	Clackmannanshire		Nairn	Dunbartonshire, East
Dumfriesshire	Dumfriesshire		Ross and Cromarty	Dunbartonshire, West
Edinburghshire	Dunbartonshire		Sky and Lochalsh	Dundee
Elginshire	East Lothian		Sutherland	Edinburgh
Fife	(Haddingtonshire until 1921)		Clackmannan	Falkirk
Forfarshire	Fife	CENTRAL	Falkirk	Fife
Haddingtonshire	Inverness-shire		Stirling	Glasgow
Inverness-shire	Kincardineshire		Annandale and Eskdale	Highland
Kincardineshire	Kinross-shire	DUMFRIES	Nithsdale	Inverclyde
Kinross-shire	Kirkcudbrightshire	AND	Stewartry	Lanarkshire, North
Kirkcudbrightshire	Lanarkshire	GALLOWAY	Wigtown	Lothian, East
Lanarkshire	Midlothian		(originally Merrick)	Lothian, West
Linlithgowshire	(Edinburghshire until 1890)		Berwickshire	Midlothian
Nairnshire	Moray	BORDERS	Ettrick and Lauderdale	Moray
Peeblesshire	(Elginshire until 1918)		Roxburgh	Na h-Eileanan Siar
Perthshire	Nairnshire		Tweeddale	Orkney
Renfrewshire	Orkney		ArgylL and Bute	Perth and Kinross
Ross-shire	Peeblesshire		(originally Argyll)	Renfrewshire
Roxburghshire	Perthshire		Bearsden and Milngavie	Renfrewshire, East
Selkirkshire	Renfrewshire		Clydebank	Scottish Borders
Stirlingshire	Ross and Cromarty		Clydesdale	Shetland
Sutherland	Roxburghshire		(originally Lanark: renamed 1980)	South Lanarkshire
Wigtownshire	Selkirkshire		Cumbernauld and Kilsyth	Sterling
	Stirlingshire	STRATHCLYDE	(originally Cumbernauld)	
	Sutherland		Cumnock and Doon Valley	
	West Lothian		Cunninghame	
	(Linlithgowshire until 1921)		Dumbarton	
	Wigtownshire		East Kilbride	
	Zetland		Eastwood	
	(Shetland)		Glasgow, City of	
			Hamilton	
			Inverclyde	
			Kilmarnock and Loudoun	
			Kyle and Carrick	
			Monklands	
			Motherwell	
			Renfrew	
			Strathkelvin	
			(Originally Bishopbriggs and Kirkintilloch)	
		TAYSIDE	Angus	
			Dundee, City of	
			Perth and Kinross	
		FIFE	Dunfermline	
			Kirkcaldy	
			North East Fife	
		LOTHIAN	East Lothian	
			Edinburgh, City of	
			Midlothian	
			West Lothian	
		ORKNEY	ORKNEY	
		SHETLAND	SHETLAND	
		WESTERN ISLES	WESTERN ISLES	

(1) NOTE: County/District names for pre-1890 and post 1890 to 1975 were sourced using: https://en.wikipedia.org/wiki/Shires_of_Scotland

(2) NOTE: County/District names for post 1975 to 1996 and Scotland's Regions were sourced using: https://en.wikipedia.org/wiki/Local_government_areas_of_Scotland_(1975-1996)

APPENDIX B
Index Key to Surname Records Location and Suggested Tartans

	DISTRICT		DISTRICT
1	Aberdeen, City of (*)	46	Kincardine and Deeside (*)
2	Aberdeenshire (*)	47	Kincardineshire (*) (2) (46)
3	Angus (*)	48	Kinross shire (*) (Kinross)
4	Annandale and Eskdale (*) (21) (36)	49	Kirkcudbrightshire (*) (21) (36)
5	Argyll (*)	50	Lanarkshire (*) (Lanark)
6	Argyll and Bute (*) (5)	51	Largs (*)
7	Arran (*)	52	Lochaber (*)
8	Ayrshire (*)	53	Lorne (*) (5)
9	Badenoch and Strathspey (*)(85)	54	Mar (*) (2)
10	Banff and Buchan (*)	55	Mentieth (*)
11	Banffshire (*)	56	Midlothian (*)
12	Berwickshire (*)	57	Monklands (*) (83)
13	Buchan (*)	58	Moray (*) Elginshire)
14	Bute (*)	59	Montrose (*)
15	Caithness (*)	60	Motherwell (*) (Lanark)
16	Carrick (*)	61	Mull (*) (79)
17	Clackmannanshire (*) (Falkirk) (68) (81)	62	Musselburgh (*)
18	Culloden (*)	63	Nairnshire (*) (Nairn)
19	Dumbarton (*)	64	Nithsdale (*)
20	Dunbartonshire (*)	65	Orkney (*)
21	Dumfriesshire (36)	66	Paisley (*)
22	Dunbar (*)	67	Peeblesshire (*)
23	Dundee, City of (*)	68	Perth (*) and Kinross
24	Dunfermline (*)	69	Perthshire (*)
25	East Kilbride (*)	70	Renfrew (*)
26	East Lothian (*)	71	Renfrewshire (*)
27	Eastwood (*) (83)	72	Ross and Cromarty (*) (15) (23) (63) (83) (86)
28	Edinburgh, City of (*)	73	Ross-shire (*) (15) (23) (63) (83) (86)
29	Edinburghshire (*) (28)	74	Rothesay (*)
30	Eglinton (*)	75	Roxburgh (*)
31	Ettrick and Lauderdale (*)	76	Roxburghshire (*) (75)
32	Falkirk (*)	77	Selkirkshire (*) (Selkirk)
33	Fife (*)	78	Shetland (Zetland) (*)
34	Fort William (*)	79	Skye and Lochalsh (*) (Isle of Skye)
35	Gala Water (*) (Gallowater)	80	St. Andrews (*)
36	Galloway (*)	81	Stirling (*)
37	Glasgow, City of (*)	82	Stirlingshire (*) (Stirling)
38	Glen Lyon (*)	83	Strathclyde (*)
39	Glen Orchy (*) (5)	84	Strathearn (*)
40	Hawick (*)	85	Strathspey (*)
41	Highland (*) (15) (23) (63) (83) (86)	86	Sutherland (*)
42	Huntly (*)	87	Tweedside (*)
43	Inverclyde (*) (71)	88	West Lothian (*)
44	Inverness (*)	89	Wigtownshire (*) (21) (36)
45	Inverness-shire (*) (44)		

TARTAN INFORMATION KEY:

(*) = A tartan by this region's name exists and is the tartan suggested for wear.
(See Appendix C for details)

(*) (##) = The 1st ()=A tartan is identified. The 2nd ()= A district tartan, listed on this page, that is suggested for wear.
(See Appendix C for details)

(*) (Name) = A tartan is identified but not one found on this page.
(See Appendix C for details)

OTHER TARTANS:

The Scottish National and Caledonian Tartans may both be substituted for any of the tartans suggested here.

Universal tartans for non-Scots are Highland Granite, Isle of Skye, and Black Watch

APPENDIX C
Scottish District/Regional Tartans
(SOURCE: https://tartanregister.gov.uk/)

Aberdeen – Circa 1782. It was apparently produced during the days of prohibition (1746-1782). A second district tartan, dated 2012, is 'Aberdeen Forever' which was designed as a modern, contemporary tartan for the City of Aberdeen.

Aberdeenshire – Commissioned by the Aberdeenshire Council in 2013 as part of its creative cultural placement program. One must apply to the Aberdeenshire Council for a non-exclusive licensing agreement to wear/use/weave this tartan

Angus – Circa 1880. It may have been originally regarded as a clan/family tartan, but it is now firmly established as a district tartan.

Argyll – Circa 1819, Argyll is both a surname and the name of an old Scottish county, Argyllshire. There is also a reference to an Argyll tartan in a letter of 1798.

Arran – Circa 1880. There are two tartans for this district: 'Arran (1880)' and 'Arran (Pendleton)' (no known date)

Ayrshire – Tartan date – 1985. Designed and copyrighted by Dr Phillip D Smith for 'Ayrshire folk who have no family tartan' - at the suggestion of the Cunninghams and Boyds who did not want their tartans being used as 'district' tartans. Although initially categorized as 'Fashion' in the absence of any documentation of 'official' acceptance, it has been re-categorized as 'District' due to common usage.

Ballater – Tartan dates to 1963 and is considered a Fashion tartan.

Ballintrae – Tartan dates to 2002. This tartan is considered a Fashion tartan.

Banff and Buchan District – Designed for the district of Banff and Buchan in 1995.

Banffshire – Tartan dates to 2021 and called 'Shades of Banffshire.' The tartan my only be purchased through the designer.

Berwickshire – Tartan dates to 2018 and is considered a Fashion tartan. Permission to weave this tartan must be gained in writing from the International Tartans or ReTweed (a registered charity).

Buchan – Tartan dated 1965. This is both a District and a Clan/Family tartan. Said by the Clan Chief, David Buchan of Auchmacoy, to have been adopted by the Buchan family around 1965 because of their long association with the Cummings which began with the marriage of Margaret, daughter of King Edgar, to William Coymen, sheriff of Forfar in 1210. The name, Buchan, though a family name, is territorial in origin.

Bute – There are nine tartans each considered a Fashion tartan, they are 'Bute (2004),' 'Bute Heather (2007),' 'Bute Heather, Ancient (2007),' 'Bute Heather, Autumn (2007),' 'Bute Heather, Black (2007),' 'Bute Heather, Grey (2007),' 'Bute Heather, Midnight (2007),' 'Bute Heather, Modern (2007),' and 'Bute Heather, Weathered (2007).'

Caledonia – Tartan dates to 1786. Caledonia is another name for Scotland. Those Scots not affiliated with a clan or not having a regional tartan would wear this one.

Caithness – Tartan dates to 1995.

Carrick – Circa 1930. The name Carrick has a Gaelic derivation ('rock') and may refer to the island of Ailsa Craig off the Ayrshire coast.

Culloden – Circa 1746. Worn by a member of Prince Charles' staff during the battle but it is not known with which family or district it was first connected.

Dunbar – Circa 1840. The tartan is known as 'Dunbar Ancient'

Dunbarton – Tartan dates to 1998 and may only be worn with the designer's consent even though for use by anyone from or associated with the County of Dunbartonshire. The spelling of Dun or Dum has changed over the years.

Dunbartonshire – Tartan dates to 1998. Must have designer's consent.

Dundee District – Based on the design of a tartan Jacket said to have been worn by Prince Charles Edward Stuart at Culloden - earliest date 1746. <u>Dundee #2</u> - Wilson's 1819 similar. Wilson's of Bannockburn a weaving firm founded c1770 near Stirling. Scottish Tartan Society archive. <u>Dundee (2003)</u> - A modern weave of the Dundee using only six colors instead of the customary seven or eight. Orange used in place of red. Sample in Scottish Tartans Authority's Dalgety Collection.

Dunfermline – Tartan date is 2001. This tartan is considered a Fashion tartan.

Edinburgh, City of – Tartan date is 2001. This is a District tartan.

East Kilbride – There are two listed tartans, 'East Kilbride #1' (1990) and 'East Kilbride #2' (no date)

East Lothian – Tartan is dated 1999. Anyone may wear this tartan only with the designer's consent.

Ettrick and Lauderdale – Tartan date is 1900, however, it is believed the tartan may have been around since the 1830's. The design may well have been based on the Wallace clan tartan which has a yellow line on black instead of the red. Ettrick is located on the river Ettrick in south Selkirkshire.

Eglinton – Tartan date is 1707.

Falkirk – Tartan is dated 1990. The original Falkirk 'Tartan' now in the National Museum of Scotland, has a place in history as one of the earliest examples of Scottish cloth in existence. It is a direct link back to the Roman occupation of the area around 250 A.D. The present day Falkirk District Tartan is alive with vibrant color to reflect that part of Scotland as it is seen today.

Fife– Tartan date is 1998. This tartan may only be worn with the designer's consent.

Fort William – Tartan date is 1819. Fort William is located on the Caledonian Canal and Loch Linnie.

Gallowater (Gala Water) – The Gallowater New district tartan, sometimes referred to as the 'Gala Water' was first mentioned in the records of Wilson's of Bannockburn in 1793. The design progressed until 1819 when a 'New' sett was recorded in the company's pattern book with a red band and a thin white stripe. Both 'Old' and 'New' tartans appear in Wilson's 1819 pattern book. The names 'Gallowater' and 'Gala Water' seem to be interchangeable, and which is used seems to depend on the source.

Galloway – Tartan date is 1950. Designed by Councillor John Hannay c1949-50.

Glasgow, City of – There are two district tartans, 'Glasgow' (1790) and 'Glasgow #2" (undated)

Glen Lyon – There are two district tartans dating back to 1819-1820.

Glen Orchy – Tartan date is 1819.

Grampian – Tartan date is 1995. Designed as a district tartan to reflect the colors of the Grampian mountains.

Hawick – There are three tartans for this district. The first, designed by Robin Deas and Kenneth Hood and adapted and woven by Andrew Elliot of Andrew Elliot Ltd, Forest Mill, Galashiels, Scotland. It was launched at a civic reception in Hawick as the official district tartan in 1996. The second, dated 1997, is the dress version of the Hawick Tartan. The Hawick Dress tartan was commissioned by the Hawick Tartan Company Ltd and designed and woven by Wrights of Trowmill. The third, dated 2003, is from the Scottish Tartans Authority's Dalgety Collection labelled 'Hawick Trade Sett SB 105C'. No information is known about this tartan, but it is based on the Royal Stewart.

Huntly – Tartan date is 1819. The Huntly district tartan is known to have been worn at the time of the '45 rebellion by Brodies, Forbes', Gordons, MacRaes, Munros and Rosses which gives a strong indication of the greater antiquity of the 'District' setts compared to the Clan tartans.

Inverness – Tartan date 1829. There are three district tartans, however, the Inverness Basque may only be worn by The Highland Council. Originally woven for the Earl of Inverness sometime prior to 1822. The territorial designation of this Royal tartan makes it appropriate for use as a district tartan.

Isle of Sky – Tartan date is 1992. This tartan requires permission from the designer to wear, Mrs. Rosemary Nicolson Samios. The designer is an Australian of Sky descent, now living in Skye. Weaver Angus MacLeod from Lewis was the first to produce commercial quantities in traditional kilt weight. Mrs. Samios controls the rights to the production of this 'Isle of Skye' district tartan through registration with the Patents Office and Lochcarron of Scotland has been appointed as the supplier of fabrics and woven accessories in this tartan.

Kincardine and Deeside – There are three tartans listed, 'City of Kincardine' (1987), 'Deeside Plaid (Taobh Dhi)' (1963), and 'Deeside, Royal' (2003).

Kinross – There are two tartans listed, 'Kinross' (2002) and 'Pride of Kinross' (2015) both classified as Fashion tartans.

Kirkaldy – Tartan date is 2008. Tartan may only be prepared for weaving by House of Tartan.

Lanark – There are two tartans listed, 'Lanark Highlands (dated 1999) a township' and 'Lanarkshire (dated 1998).' The latter has wear restrictions in that you must have the designer's consent.

Lanarkshire – There are three tartans listed, 'Lanarkshire' (1998), 'South Lanarkshire' (2001), and 'Spirit of South Lanarkshire' (no date)

Largs – Tartan date is 1983.

Lochaber – Tartan date is 1797. The origin of this tartan is uncertain, and it now generally is accepted as a district tartan.

Mentieth – Tartan date is 2002.

Midlothian – Tartan date is 1998. May be worn only with designer's consent.

Montrose – there are two district tartans: 'Montrose (Macnaughton variation)' (dated 1986) and 'Montrose of Alabama" (dated 1996)

Moray – tartan believed to be dated to the early 19th century.

Mull – Tartan believed to have been woven in 1819. How this tartan came to named 'Mull' is not recorded.

Musselburgh – Tartan dates to 1956.

Nairn – There are two tartans named, 'Nairn' (1930) and 'Nairn (Edinburgh Woollen Mill)' (2002). The latter is classified as a Fashion tartan.

Nithsdale – There are two tartans dating to 1930 and 2002. Both versions require permission to be worn.

Orkney – There are five Orkney tartans, each is considered a "Fashion Tartan" as no official local recognition of these has been given. Blue Brough from Orkney (2011), Orkney (2000), Orkney Slate (2011), Heather (2014), and Magnus (2014).

Paisley – Tartan dates to 1952. The tartan has also come to be regarded as a family tartan for those of the name Paisley.

Peebleshire – Tartan dates to 2000. Listed as 'Peebles Beltane Centenary' with the full name stated as 'Royal Burgh of Peebles Centenary Tartan'

Perth – Tartan dates to 2017 and is listed as 'Perth County'

Perthshire – Tartan date 1831. 'Perthshire or Drummond of Perth.' Also known as the 'Perthshire Rock & Wheel.' The sett is said to be a variation of a pattern called 'Stewart of Fingask', after a plaid allegedly left by Prince Charles Edward Stuart at Fingask in Perthshire in 1746.

Renfrew – There are two tartans listed, 'Renfrew' and 'Renfrew #2'. Both are dated as 2002 and classified as Fashion tartans.

Renfrewshire – Tartan date is 1998. This tartan may only be worn by anyone from this county but must have the designer's consent.

Rothesay – There are three district tartans listed: 'Rothesay,' (dating to 2002), 'Rothesay #2' (dating to 1906), and 'Rothesay Hunting, Duke of '(dating to 1897).

Roxburgh – There are two tartans for this district: 'Roxburgh' (dating to 1952) and 'Roxburgh Red' (dating to 1840).

Selkirk – This district tartan was designed by Andrew Elliot of Andrew Elliot Ltd, Forest Mill, Selkirk, Scotland. 29th March 1996.

Shetland – Tartan date is 2017. 'The Spirit of Shetland' depicts the landscape of Shetland. Colors; grey and green represent the land; purple represents heather; blues for the sea and sky; yellow for the sandy beaches. This tartan can only be woven with the permission of Aurora Orkney Ltd.

St. Andrews – Tartan date is 2003.

Stirling – Listed as Stirling and Bannockburn, this tartan dates to 1847. In 1987 the Stirling and Bannockburn Dress tartan was woven (and designed) by D MacArthur & Company of Glasgow.

Strathclyde – There are three district tartans listed: 'Strathclyde' (undated), 'Strathclyde (Official)' (dated 1975), and 'Strathclyde Blue' (dated 1993).

Strathearn – There are two district tartans listed: 'Strathearn' (dated 1820) and 'Crieff & Strathearn #1' (dated 1988).

Strathspey – This district tartan is listed as 'Strathspey Estate Check.' There is no date provided. There are two other tartans listed for Strathspey, the first called "18th Century Military Tartan from Strathspey" which dates to 1794. This tartan has been erroneously called the Strathspey district tartan. The second is called "Strathspey" and is classified as a Fashion Tartan dating to 1975.

Stirling & Bannockburn – There are two district tartans listed: Stirling and Bannockburn' (dated 1847) and 'Stirling & Bannockburn Dress' (dated 1987)

Sutherland – There are two district tartans listed. The first, officially named the 'Strath Hallidale (Sutherland)' (1998). The second named the Sutherland #2 (2002) which is the same as the Black Watch but usually woven in lighter shades with azure replacing the dark blue of the Black Watch. As worn by the Argyll and Sutherland Highlanders it is kilted to show the green, whereas with the Black Watch it is kilted to show the blue.

Tweedside –There are two district tartans listed: 'Tweedside Red' (dated 1840) and 'Tweedside Hunting' (dated 1968)

West Lothian – Tartan dated 1998. For use by anyone from or associated with the County of Linlithgowshire, now West Lothian. Must have the designer's consent.

APPENDIX D
Source Information

1. *The Surnames of Scotland, Their Origin, Meaning & History by George F. Black with Mary Elder Black. Published by Churchill & Dunn Ltd. First Printing 1946.*

2. Directory of Scots Banished to the American Plantations 1650 – 1775, Second Edition, by David Dobson. Published by Clearfield Company, Baltimore, Maryland. First published in 1983.

3. The National Library of Australia, Convict Transportation Registers, 1787 – 1870, Canberra: Australian Joint Copying Project (digitized). Author: Great Britain, Home Office.

4. *A Dictionary of English Surnames*, first published 1958, third edition, with corrections and additions, published 1991 - Routledge, by PH. Reaney Litt.D., Ph.D., F.S.A. & R.M. Wilson, M.A.

5. *Tartan For Me!* 9th Edition, by Philip D. Smith, Jr., Ph.D.

6. Scottish Prisoners and their Relocation (https://www.geni.com/projects/Scots-Prisoners-and-their-Relocation-to-the-Colonies-1650-1654/3465)

7. *Scottish DISTRICT/Regional Tartans (https://www.tartanregister.gov.uk/)*

8. Scottish Census records 1841 through 1922 (https://www.scotlandspeople.gov.uk/guides/census-returns)

9. Directory of Scots Banished to the American Plantations, 1650-1775 (https://www.ancestry.com/search/collections/48517/)

10. The Church of Jesus Christ of Latter-Day Saints (LDS) index 1841 through 1911 (https://www.scotlandspeople.gov.uk/guides/census-returns#1881%20(LDS%20index)

11. *Scottish Prisoners of War Society (https://spows.org/battle_of_dunbar_pows_america/). As of 28 Dec 2022, the site was marked for deletion due to many links on the page not working.*

12. *National Registers of Scotland, Catholic Parish Registers (1553 – 1854) (https://www.nrscotland.gov.uk/research/guides/catholic-parish-registers)*

13. *Historic Guide to Scottish Districts (https://www.nrsscotland.gov.uk/files//research/statutory-registers/registration-districts-of-scotland-guide.pdf)*

14. *Shires of Scotland (https://en.wikipedia.org/wiki/Shires_of_Scotland)*

15. *County/District names for post 1975 to 1996 and Scotland's Regions (https://en.wikipedia.org/wiki/Local_government_areas_of_Scotland_(1975-1996))*

16. *Scotland's People (www.scotlandspeople.gov.uk)*

17. *Surnames of Scotland and Clan Territories of Scotland (https://www.origenesmaps.com/maps) and (www.scottishorigenes.com) by Tyrone Bowes, PhD.*

18. *Family Tree Y-DNA Project (https://www.familytreedna.com/groups/scottish-po-ws/about/background)*

19. *The Scots In Australia 1788 – 1938, by Benjamin Wilkie, 2017, Boydell Press*

APPENDIX E
Sites of Interest

1. *www.ellisisland.org*
   The Ellis Island Foundation

2. *www.nationalarchives.gov.uk*
   the UK National Archives, UK Vital Records

3. *www.archives.gov/research/genealogy*
   US National Archives and Records Administration

4. *https://www.genealogybank.com*
   Mormon Genealogy Bank

Printed in the United States
by Baker & Taylor Publisher Services